Peggy Cole's

TASTE OF THE COUNTRY
SEASONS

MORROW & CO.
BUNGAY, SUFFOLK
1996

First published Morrow & Co, Bungay, 1996

ISBN 0948903 48 1

Designed & typeset by Morrow & Co, Bungay, Suffolk
Printed and bound by St Edmundsbury Press

FOREWORD

As a long time admirer of Peggy Cole, and for twenty years a near neighbour, I was happy to contribute a recipe to her new book, despite the fact that she is a far better cook than I shall ever be.

Peggy has written several books about Suffolk life and her many and varied interests. Her garden is famous in the county, and beyond its borders, and she donates a substantial sum from her 'openings' to charity each year.

Cooking and Wine making are among her many accomplishments, and it seems right for her to make this collection of recipes for publication.

Peggy is a true 'countryman' in every sense of the word. Born and brought up in a rural and at times tough environment, she has used all her talents to the full, based on long experience, and a love of nature and the countryside of her beloved Suffolk. To entertain Her Royal Highness The Princess Margaret to tea in her cottage, which she has done, was as natural to her as it would have been to do the same for her next door neighbour.

I am sure that this collection of recipes compiled by Peggy Cole will be another well worth addition to the bookshelves of many keen cooks in Suffolk and beyond.

Lady Penn

Carnbee House,
Anstruther,
Fife
May 1996

DEDICATION

To my brother, Ronnie Balls, for all his help in the garden at Akenfield, and for his kindness over the years.

ACKNOWLEDGEMENTS

Once again I would like to thank all my many friends from far and wide, also my readers from the *East Anglian Daily Times* and BBC Suffolk Radio listeners. Special thanks to the Duchess of Devonshire, Lady Maclean and Lady Penn for allowing me to use their favourite recipes in my book, and to Helen Southwood for her beautiful drawings.

In putting this book together I had invaluable assistance from my agent, secretary and friend, Evelyn Curtis, who spent many hours typing the manuscript, and edited it with the utmost care and sympathy for my ideas, giving me encouragement and support along the way. I am very grateful to her.

Peggy Cole

Akenfield,
Charsfield,
Suffolk
May 1996

Contents

		page
Foreword	*by Lady Penn*	(iii)
Introduction		1
Winter		7
Spring		25
Summer		55
Autumn		124
Index of recipes		152

Illustrations

page

Peggy & the M.B.E. Cake   3

Peggy meeting H.R.H. Princess Margaret   4

Winter: drawn by Helen Southwood   7

Spring: drawn by Helen Southwood   25

Biscuit making: Sarah & Russell   30

Patrick Anthony, Peggy & Akenfield Cake   31

Summer: drawn by Helen Southwood   55

A selection of baking, preserves & wine   67

Evelyn & Peggy at work on the book   68

Home made preserves   107

Autumn: drawn by Helen Southwood   124

Fresh from Akenfield Garden for chutney making   127

Peggy Cole's Taste of the Country Seasons

Living in the country, in fact a small country village, the seasons of the year have, in many ways, had a great effect on my life. More so probably than it has for our friends, who live in towns and certainly those who live in cities. Whereas they are often woken up in the morning by the sound of traffic and people, the alarm clock which I remember most of all, is the sound of the cockerel, as he welcomes the sun, or the noise of farm animals ready and eager to be fed. There were times, especially in spring and summer, when the first sound that came through the bedroom window was that of the dawn chorus as, one after the other, the birds woke up and began to vie with each other for territorial rights from the first sign of light. Things have changed, even in the rural scene, where many of the old sounds and sights have been taken over by others, but still there is a peacefulness and serenity that never changes and which makes me glad to be, although older, but whether wiser may be open to dispute, very much a country girl.

Born and brought up in a small village in the heart of Suffolk, my life has been governed by the lore and tradition of the village. It is these things which will be the recurring theme as we look through the various stages and periods of the year as they affect my life. The old country sayings ridiculed by some and yet still possessing a value and worth even after so many years.

Perhaps I have been fortunate in a lot of ways. I was taught from early in my life, the value of nature in its wider setting, and so I developed a real love for gardening. Producing beautiful flowers and vegetables is a delight which has grown with the years, and I am still constantly amazed as I watch things grow and develop during the seasons. Of course, nowadays it is quite difficult to keep in touch with the many new and upgraded varieties and methods, all designed for easier gardening, but for me there is still a lot to be said for the old-fashioned ways of doing things. Nothing can take the place of deep digging and constant use of the hoe and, as many of my friends will confirm, I am not called 'the muck lady' for nothing! In my mind, no amount of artificial means can ever replace the good nutrition obtained from farmyard manure. There is nothing better than to go into the garden first thing in the morning, especially in spring or early summer, and drink in the sounds and sights that are all around me. The dew on the grass, the jewels of water nestling in the centre of tiny flowers and the songs of the blackbird and thrush as they forage to get the first meal of the day. As evening draws in and the light begins to fade, again this is a wonderful time just to sit and relax and let the hard work of the day gradually fall away. The scents are different at this time of the day and it always seems that as the warmth of the evening bathes the flowers, somehow the perfume is stronger from the night-scented stocks, pinks, carnations and roses. The sound of birdsong gives place very gradually to the drone of the insect world and stillness once again returns - broken sadly, today, by sounds more mechanical than natural. It's easy to see the truth in the old saying, and there will be many of these in the following pages, that 'you are nearer God's heart in a garden than anywhere else on earth'.

For many people it may not appear to be a blessing to have been brought up knowing what it was to go without. Yet, as I look back to my childhood, I realise now that many of the things that I do, stem from those early days. There were the times of 'make-do and mend' and this was never more true than in the food we ate and the way it was prepared. Even now, to waste any food seems

The W.I. Market at Woodbridge made this cake and gave it to me the week I got my M.B.E.

Peggy meeting H.R.H. Princess Margaret at the Suffolk Show in May 1995

to me to be a sin. Consequently a lot of the recipes which are dotted throughout the book, are ones which use ordinary everyday ingredients that are easy to produce, and delicious to eat. I'm an old-fashioned countrywoman and do not claim to be a culinary expert, and I was brought up with the problem of making ends meet. Fortunately, my hobbies of gardening and cooking both combine with each other. With the bounty of the countryside, I like to make use of the fruits for wine and preserves. Over the years I have made so many friends and my telephone is constantly ringing, with people calling who have problems relating to gardening, cookery and folklore. With this book I have tried to give you a mixture of what, to me, started out as hobbies, but have now become a part of my life. I have included many of the recipes which I have enjoyed making, and it is a double pleasure as, so often, I have grown the vegetables and made a meal from my own garden.

Readers of my articles over the years have been most kind and sent me hints etc., and I hope that you will find them as useful as I have. Let growing and preparing food be one of your favourite leisure activities and you will have the satisfaction of getting the best value for money - what more can you ask of any hobby.

Not only have many things changed outside in the garden, but times have changed in our kitchens as well. It used to be the old cooking ranges, and a good job they did, but they had their problems. The trouble was that if the wind was blowing from the wrong direction, the ovens would not heat. Mind you, it could also work the other way - then, they would get so hot that cakes or bread would burn. I can remember my mother using a double-burner oil stove on which she put a portable oven. It was slow, but some lovely cakes came out of that oven. Today, modern electric kitchens have surface cooking units built into cabinet tops, and ovens recessed into the wall. Temperature controls for both of these very convenient features are at eye level. Gas stoves come equipped with two ovens, a broiler and often an automatic time clock, while a pilot light ignites the gas without having to resort to a match every time you want to use it. How lucky we all are today now that most cooking is done purely by pressing a switch. If you happen to have unexpected callers it is always nice to have a freshly baked cake in your cake tin, and here is my first recipe for a good old-fashioned spicy cake.

Spicy Malt Loaf Cake

Ingredients

8oz wholemeal flour
2oz dark soft brown sugar
8oz mixed dried fruit
2 tablespoons golden syrup
2 tablespoons malt extract
1 teaspoon cinnamon
1 teaspoon nutmeg
1 egg
$1/4$ pint milk

Method

Pre-heat oven to 325°F/170°C or Gas 3 with a shelf set at the centre. Grease and line with greaseproof paper a 2lb loaf tin or an 8" round cake tin.

Winter

Mix the flour, sugar, mixed fruit and a pinch of salt in a bowl. Make a well in the centre and pour in the syrup, malt extract, egg and milk. Mix these wet ingredients together, then gradually mix in the dry ingredients and beat thoroughly until smooth. Put the mixture into the prepared tin and bake for about $1^1/4$ hours. Leave to cook in the tin. This cake is also nice sliced and buttered, and its even nicer stored in an airtight tin for at least a day, it freezes well too.

Of all the seasons, to me, the one which I like least, is I suppose, winter. The colours and smells of summer flowers and fruits are gone and the charm of autumn shades, which change daily as the trees shake off their foliage, leaving us with a feeling of emptiness. It still seems a long time ahead before we can enjoy the newness of springtime when everything will again come to life. The November nights are long and dark, and herald more weeks of the same, and the fogs and cold wet weather always seems to chill through to the bone and bring with them a sense of depression.

Even December, although we can get days of fitful sunshine, isn't much better and the best one can say is that we are one month nearer spring with the promise that it brings. There is a saying about the month of December that it takes away everything and returns nothing, and there is a lot of truth in it, certainly so far as the garden is concerned. As in nature, when everything is dormant and asleep, so it is with us; we get that 'can't be bothered' feeling all too quickly and it always seems to be so much easier to put off doing those jobs which ought to be done, until tomorrow. At least, that's how I feel and I don't think that I am alone, although there are many jobs which have to be done, however we feel, and however much we want to keep indoors in the warm. One problem is, that because of the short amount of daylight, it is often difficult to fit in these necessary tasks unless the temptations are overcome. One such job is catching up with the last of the winter digging. This ought to be done by the end of December and certainly by the early part of January, then the soil can be left in sizeable clods of earth which can be broken down by the frosts when they come. Talking about digging, if you are putting compost or manure on the land, now is the time that it should be dug in before the hard frost sets in.

For some reason there seems not to be the marked differences today as there used to be between the seasons, so far as the weather is concerned. It doesn't seem as cold, generally speaking, during the winter months, as once it did, and I am sure that we do not see as much snow as we did when I was a child. The one thing that doesn't change very much, at least where I live, is the cold east wind. That is still as cold and bitter as ever it was, and although it can be quite stingy at any time during the year, in winter time it really makes its presence felt when there is no warm sun to temper it. The older people call this wind a lazy wind because it doesn't bother to go round you, but seems to go straight through the body instead, and anyone who has experienced its bitterness will know that the old saying makes a lot of sense.

Yet winter isn't all bad and there are some things which it brings that have their own attraction. On a cold and wet winter's evening it is nice to be able to close one's door on the weather and sit in front of a lovely warm fire, especially when you can do so without feeling guilty because of all the other tasks you should be doing outside. Although the majority of people have central heating to warm their rooms, I still have an old-fashioned open fireplace, even if it does take a lot more effort to keep it clean and sometimes, to get it started. To me there is nothing better than sitting and watching the burning coals as they make their strange patterns in the fireplace, or see the shadows cast by the flames on walls and ceilings as they dance about in the darkness of the room before the light is switched on. Perhaps this method of warming does mean that whilst the fire makes your feet hot, your back still feels cold, especially when the wind is on the wrong side of the house. I still prefer a nice coal fire to the modern way, and its certainly better to look at than radiators.

Then there is Christmas, the time of the year when we all eat and drink too much but never really worry about it. On a serious note, there is the lovely idea that everyone thinks about other people more than they do themselves. I think that the reason for this is because of what Christmas celebrates - the coming of the tiny babe to Bethlehem - but whatever the thought behind it, it's a good one and what a great pity that often it only lasts for those few days. Christmas might be more for the children, but I, for one, love it and everything that goes into it. The decorations and holly hung around the room, the parties, when we often have friends in for a mince pie and a glass of homemade wine, the cards and presents, it's magic! It's a special time in so many ways, and even if it isn't quite like it was in the old days when I was a girl, it still means a lot to me.

Today children don't often have to wait for this one day in the year to have presents, like it was when we were young. Christmas morning could never come quickly enough for us, and long before our parents were up and about, we would be awake to see if Father Christmas had been and whether or not he had left anything for us in the sock which had been left carefully fixed to the rail at the bottom of the bed the night before. Usually, there would be a few small items in it, like an orange or some nuts and a colouring book with some crayons, not much by today's standards, but wonderful in our eyes. Then downstairs, where the main presents would be waiting for us - just one - not a shopful which some children receive today, but that one was valued and played with over and over again, for days and weeks to come.

In the country areas particularly, old sayings and country lore abound, and it is quite easy to find one or another which correspond with any time of the year. Many of the superstitions which our forefathers lived by can be seen to be appropriate, even in these modern times. Although to those younger and more sophisticated, many of the old-fashioned ideas are no more than country tales and have no place in today's world. It only takes a little thought to see that this is not really the case and that those ideas which governed the way our parents and grandparents lived, were not a lot of twaddle but had in fact been thought out by a careful study of weather and other circumstances. Take, for example, sayings like 'If you see grass in January, lock your grain in the granary', or 'January warm, let the Lord have mercy'. These show the danger of being taken in by the prospect of good weather too early in the year. Many a gardener has found the truth of the saying that 'when January commits its fault, it is May that bears the blame'. Not only is a warning sounded in these sayings, but there are those which give good advice as well. 'When oak trees bend with snow in January, good crops may be expected', so that although no-one really likes the cold weather, snows and frosts, which are a part of winter, they are in fact necessary if in the succeeding months good crops can follow.

Another saying about January is that 'it is the blackest month of the year, in which the first three days rule the first three months while the last twelve days of January are said to govern the weather for the whole of the year'. One quaint saying which I came across, is that 'January is like a gentleman; as he begins, so he goes on'. Not only is there an abundance of country sayings, some of which have undoubtedly been adopted by the townspeople, the same could be said of rites and customs. There are a number of interesting ones connected with the New Year and Twelfth Night. One such was that of wassailing the fruit trees, and this was believed to charm the trees and make them produce a good crop in the following season. Originally dating from way back, this usually took place on the 17th January, although it has been carried out as early as the 6th of the month. It was the time when a drink called 'lamb's wool' and made up from roasted apples, sugar, ginger, nutmeg, cinnamon and wine or ale, was prepared and put into the wassail bowl. The bowl was then carried to the orchard where a toast was given and echoed by all the farmers and their workers. The remains of the wassail was poured over the trees and a gun fired several times in order to drive away any lurking evil spirits. As this was done, the following rhyme was chanted :-

> *Old apple tree, old apple tree,*
> *We have come to wassail thee,*
> *To bear and to bow apples now,*
> *Hats full, caps full,*
> *Three bushel bags full,*
> *Barn floors full,*
> *And a little heap under the stairs.*

No doubt we get cold weather this month and there are some foods which are particularly appropriate. Ham bones and meat, which have been left over from the festive season can often be found in the larder. I never throw mine away in the dustbin or to the birds, as this is the time of the year to get the soup pan on the go. What about **pea soup** - I think its name could have been taken from the thick fogs that were once a regular feature of winter. The day before you think of having this good wholesome food, some dried peas, butter beans, haricot beans and lentils need to be soaked in a bowl of water. My mother used to put a pinch of bicarbonate of soda in with the pulses. This was supposed to be a charm against flatulence. You really need a ham or bacon bone for this soup to give it a flavour, even a knuckle of ham will do. After soaking the pulses, put them into a large pan with the ham bones. Cover with water and cook slowly for two to three hours. I also add any vegetables that are available, and these I dice and put in the mixture for the last half to three-quarters of an hour cooking time. Serve with Suffolk Dumplings and you will find that it is as good as any high-class meal.

Later on in my book you will see that I have given recipes of the different variations for making dumplings, and don't forget that dumplings can be used as a sweet pudding, using jam, golden syrup or even lemon juice.

You can also use chestnuts to make another good soup, in fact this recipe is very useful for using up the chestnuts which are left lying around after Christmas.

For **chestnut soup** you will need:-

Ingredients

1lb chestnuts (after skinning)
1 pint milk
1 pint stock
I small onion
Few sticks of celery with seasoning

Method
Peel, chop and cook the onion very lightly in a little butter and add sufficient stock and mash to a pulp. Add the celery after cutting into small pieces, then the chestnuts and the remaining stock with the seasoning. Gently bring to the boil and simmer until soft. Rub through a sieve, or put through a food processor, return soup to the saucepan, add top of the milk, heat and serve hot.

Whilst talking about soup, I thought that you would like to hear this soup tale which was told to me by a chef at a local hotel.

'Once upon a time a tramp knocked at the door of a farmhouse and asked for something to eat, only to be told by the farmer's wife that there was nothing in the house. Refusing to take no for an answer, the tramp said that he could show her an excellent recipe for pebble soup, using only pebbles in water. Her curiosity aroused, she asked him to show her, so he picked up some stones, washed them carefully and put them in a large pot with some water, just a little salt he said and plenty of time to cook. Later, when asked how the soup was progressing, the tramp replied that it's going to be good, but it's a pity that you haven't got an onion as that would make all the difference. Not wishing to spoil the soup, the farmer's wife went and found one. Tasting the soup once more, the tramp expressed his satisfaction, but said that, of course, a carrot would have helped, but if you haven't got one, we'll just have to do without. Well, the woman did have a carrot and she even found a beef bone that she had been saving for the dog, and this was added to the mixture. At last, it was ready and as the tramp had promised, it was delicious, delicately flavoured with carrots, onion and a good beef bone. After having eaten, the tramp now refreshed, bade her farewell and set off down the road. After he had left, the farmer's wife went back into the kitchen to see if there was any more soup left in the pan, but all that remained were the pebbles, hard and stony just as they had been when they were first put in. The moral of this story is that you only get out what you put in'.

This is the time of year when we need a hot meal so what about the onion family. We grow a lot of onions and I often get asked what I do with them all, but it's rather a case of finding something which cannot be done with an onion - no matter what kind it is.

Onion skin very thin,
Mild winter coming in.
Onion skin thick and tough,
Come winter cold and rough.

I love this little verse, and each winter I look to see whether my onion skins are thin or thick. Did you know that the skins of onions make a fine yellow dye, and that if you put half of a raw onion in a bucket of cold water and place this in the centre of a freshly painted room, it will take away the smell of paint.

Eating too many badly cooked or raw onions is said to bring bad dreams, whilst fried onions for supper make people shout out in their sleep. I have also been told that to dream about onions is very unlucky. There is no doubting the truth of the saying that, 'one man's meat is another man's poison', and this is very apt when talking of onions. They should only be eaten in moderation, otherwise indigestion may well be the result.

Stuffed Onions

If you have some of the larger onions left in your store, they will make a good dish. Take them, peel and cook them whole in salted water for half to three-quarters of an hour. Scoop out the centres, chop them and mix with three-quarters of a pound of minced beef (this is for about four large onions). Take also, six ounces breadcrumbs, salt and pepper and a good tablespoon of mixed herbs, such as parsley, thyme or marjoram. Bind the mixture with a beaten egg, then put all the ingredients into the part-cooked onions shells. Stand them in a dish with a little dripping and bake for about half to three-quarters of an hour at 350°F/180°C or Gas 4 until they are brown on top.

A lot can be said for a good old stew and dumplings. I remember when I came back from lecturing on the QE2, all I really wanted when I got home, after all the luxury eating, was some good plain food. There are so many ways, as well as names, for the common dumpling and, as children, we often had them as it was one way of filling us up. You very rarely had them with meat, but they would be served with a good gravy. One thing I find is that the young housewives sometimes get muddled when the recipe says hard or soft dumplings. I always think of hard dumplings as those made with 4 ozs self-raising flour; 2 ozs suet ; a good pinch of salt and about 4 tablespoons of water. Mix this to a soft dough with water and turn onto a well-floured board. Form into small balls and drop them into a stew or casserole, then replace the lid and simmer for 25 minutes. If its only soft dumplings which are needed, then I just mix 4 ozs self-raising flour with a pinch of salt and some water or, if I have an egg to spare, I will use this instead of the water. Form this mixture into small balls then drop them into the meat dish and cook for 10 minutes or so. Sometimes I mix chopped parsley in with the mixture as this gives a pleasant taste. Incidentally, these dumplings should be eaten as soon as cooked, as they tend to go hard very quickly. You can use 2 oz of margarine to your 4 oz of flour if you want a dumpling that will last another day, and stay fluffy and light. Don't forget that dumplings can also be used as a sweet pudding, using jam, golden syrup or even lemon juice.

I was given the following recipe by a Welsh visitor to my garden, and you can see why they call their dumplings 'nacker jacks'.

Leeky Stew With Nacker Jack

Ingredients

1lb trimmed leeks
3/4lb peeled potatoes
12 ozs lean bacon
1 1/2 pints of chicken stock
Pepper and salt

For the **Nacker Jack** you will need:-

Ingredients

8 ozs self-raising flour
4 ozs shredded suet
1/2 teaspoon salt and water to mix

Method

Cut the leeks into three inch lengths and wash well. Cut the potatoes and bacon into fairly large pieces and place in a four-pint ovenproof dish with the leeks, stock and seasoning. Cover and cook at 400°F/200°C or Gas Mark 6, for one hour.

Make the Nacker Jack by mixing all the ingredients to form a soft dough. Pat out on a floured surface to one inch thick. Place carefully on the stew, cover and return to the oven for a further twenty minutes, it's then ready to serve.

I wonder why so many people fight shy of the parsnip for, after a good frost when the roots have become mellow and golden, it has the sweetest of flavours. One idea is to make **parsnip chips**, and this is how I make them :-

Wash and cut into four then divide again until they are the size you would use for potato chips. Pop these into cold water for five minutes or so, then drain off the water and dry the chips thoroughly and toss them in dry flour and just fry them in the same way as chipped potatoes.

This vegetable is one from which some of the best wine can be made and the recipe that I use for **parsnip wine** is as follows:-

Ingredients

4 lb parsnips
2 3/4 lb sugar
2 lemons
1 orange
1 gallon water, and yeast and nutrient

Method

Scrub and slice the parsnips and boil together the thinly peeled rinds of the fruit in six pints of the water. Don't overboil, but just allow the parsnips to become tender, otherwise the wine will go cloudy. Strain the liquid off onto the sugar with the remaining two pints of boiling water and fruit juice. Add the yeast and nutrient when the temperature comes down to blood heat and pour into a fermentation jar. Leave the liquid until the fermenting process has finished, then rack and leave for a year if you can manage it.

The parsnip is such a versatile vegetable and so many things can be done with it. For instance, **parsnip fritters** are a delicious dish, and so easy to make.

All you need is about two pounds of cooked and mashed parsnips, with salt and pepper and a little grated nutmeg, three to four ounces of white breadcrumbs, two small beaten eggs, three ounces of flour and about two teaspoonsful chopped parsley.

Method

Put parsnips and parsley together with salt, pepper and nutmeg into a bowl. Mix well and bind with the beaten egg, then using the flour, shape with your hands into about eight or ten patties. Coat these well with flour, then dip into the egg and breadcrumbs. Fry the fritters in deep fat, turning them until they are golden brown. Serve hot.

The same basic recipe can be used for **potato cakes**, except that with these, the nutmeg is omitted and much more parsley is needed. This makes a very tasty dish and, when we were children, we were almost brought up on potato cakes. If you are soon to marry, one of the most important things to put on your wedding present list is a casserole dish, and do make sure that you find a really good one, with a well-fitting lid - these are a must in any kitchen, as they retain heat much longer than an ordinary pan, so less power is required when using them. Another thing is, that once the pan is hot there is little or no evaporation, and the full flavour of the food is retained. When I am stuck and do not know what to cook for my brother, I will often make what I call my **quick casserole**, in fact I make two or three at the same time by doubling up the ingredients. These extra ones are then frozen for use at a later date.

All that is necessary is:-

1lb onions
1lb sausages
1lb lambs liver
1/2lb streaky bacon

You will also need a few pieces of celery, some slices of carrot and a small tin of tomatoes and added salt and pepper. To top it up, use about four fluid ounces of home-made red wine.

Preparation

Skin and slice the onions, trim liver and remove bacon rinds (these can be put in the stock pot), clean and cut the celery and carrots into small pieces. Fry the onions and sausages in a little dripping until they are brown. Place layers of liver, onions, bacon, vegetables and sausages, in a casserole dish. Season with salt and pepper and a sprig of parsley. You will notice that I use a lot of parsley in my dishes, as I think it is very good for you. Empty the tomatoes over the rest of the ingredients and add the wine. Put the lid on and cook in oven 375°F/190°C or Gas Mark 5, for half to three quarters of an hour.

21

You can put a large potato in the oven to bake or you can remove the lid after 15 to 20 minutes and put in small dumplings on top of the casserole (see earlier recipe for dumplings). This is a satisfying dish on a cold day.

No sooner are the festivities of Christmas over, then I am looking for the Seville oranges, as once they appear in the shops the great marmalade season is with us. I am one of those people who don't like mincing peel, so all the gear comes out; fruit cutting boards, a basin for the pips, a pan for the shredded fruit and what is very important, a cloth for constant wiping of the fingers, and very sharp knives. I have got a shredder, but only use it when I am pushed for time, actually my brother is very useful in the winter evenings, as he will sit at the table cutting up the peel for me.

My recipe for **marmalade** is :-

Ingredients

2lbs Seville oranges
1 lemon
4lbs sugar
4 pints water (the juice will produce
about half a pint of liquid)

Method

Soak the thinly sliced peel all night, take out the pith and pips from the fruit, tie in a muslin bag and boil these with the peel for about one hour. Remove the muslin bag just before adding the sugar, then boil for about 15 minutes until the marmalade is set.

I like to boil this mixture when I can have the windows open, otherwise there is a lot of condensation. However, think of the satisfaction you will have once the jars are filled, as not only are they a welcome addition to the pantry shelves, a jar of marmalade makes a very good present for friends and relations.

Ginger marmalade can be made by adding about 4 ounces of chopped preserved ginger, which can be added 10 minutes before the end of boiling.

Of course, homemade wine can be made at any time of the year, depending upon when the necessary fruit or vegetables are available. However, some wines, such as rice or potato and wheat, can be made at any time, the latter is often known as Poor Man's Brandy.

Wine making is an interesting and absorbing hobby, and is well worth the time which it takes, especially when the finished product has been allowed to stand for perhaps a year, if you have the necessary will-power!!

Here are the recipes for these two wines:-

Rice Wine

Ingredients

3lb rice
1lb raisins
3lb sugar
1 gallon water
1 pinch isinglass and yeast

Method

Put the rice and sugar in a large container and cover with warm water. Add chopped raisins and yeast and sprinkle with the isinglass. Leave this covered for nine days before straining into a fermentation jar. Rack and bottle.

Note: This wine is a little harsh at first, so it is best to keep it for as long as possible.

Poor Man's Brandy - Potato and Wheat

Ingredients

2lb potatoes
2lb chopped raisins
1 gallon water
1lb crushed wheat
3lb demerara sugar and the rind and juice of two lemons and one orange

Method

Scrub and cut the potatoes into small pieces and, with the washed wheat, put into a large container with the raisins and thin peel from the citrus fruit. Pour on one gallon of boiling water and leave for three days, well covered. After three days, strain and squeeze, and then stir in the sugar, fruit juice and yeast. Put into a fermentation jar and leave until the fermenting process has finished, then rack and let the wine mature before bottling. If you can leave this wine for two years, the result will be delicious.

Spring

Taste of the Country Seasons

Spring makes one feel good, with sunshine getting warmer each day. Come April it's one of my favourite months. Under glass it's very pleasant working, pricking out seedlings in the greenhouse. It's also time for the first rhubarb to be pulled. Years ago every cottage had a large clump of rhubarb growing at the bottom of the garden, barrow loads of manure would have been thrown over the roots - some 2 - 3 ft high. Every spring there would emerge stick upon stick of juicy rhubarb that snapped cleanly when bent over, and it was always sweet and sour and made wonderful tarts and pies. I still say the best rhubarb is grown this way. 'Varietie Champagne' is a good plant to have and there are so many uses for this vegetable. Yes, this may surprise you, so many people think it's a fruit. You can pull it up and just wipe the stems, cut it into pieces and freeze. I make rhubarb and ginger jam and rhubarb chutney. Try using the flavour of an orange when making **rhubarb** pie, it combines well. Never eat the leaves of this plant because they contain oxalic acid which may prove poisonous. I like to make a good old-fashioned turnover by making pastry on a flat baking sheet, then cut up rhubarb into lengths of about 1 inch long, lay on the pastry and sprinkle with brown sugar, fold pastry over, damp edges to seal, then bake in a moderate oven for about 30-40 minutes.

The small things are important
Like a 'phone call or a card
To say I am thinking of you
When another's way is hard.
A friendly word, a listening ear
For those that need to share
Their burdens or their loneliness
To show them that you care.

I often get little notes from my postbag. The one above I like and I am sure many will know what those words mean when all alone. In the early part of the year we hold our village church A.G. Meetings and the same worry comes up for fund raising. Cake stalls, I feel, do the best, but it is hard work trying to get people to make you cakes or pies.

A recipe for **Walnut Tray Bake** is very popular.

Ingredients

8 ozs SR flour
4 ozs margarine
4 ozs castor sugar
3 large eggs
12 ozs chopped dates
6 ozs finely chopped walnuts

Method

Cream sugar and margarine together. Gradually add beaten eggs alternately with flour. Mix in dates and walnuts and place in greased Swiss roll tins. (You should have enough mixture for two tins 12 x 9 inch). Smooth the mixture out and bake at 350°F/180°C or Gas No. 4 for about 30 minutes. Cut into slices when cold.

Another easy loaf cake which doesn't cost too much to make is:-

Spicy Tea Cake

Ingredients

12 fluid ozs hot strong tea
7 ozs soft brown sugar
12 ozs mixed dried fruit
10 ozs S.R. flour
1¹/₂ teaspoons ground cinnamon
1 large egg

Method

Pour hot tea over sugar and fruit. When cold add flour, cinnamon, and egg. Mix well and bake in a lined 8 inch cake tin. Bake at 350°F/180°C or Gas No. 4 for about 1³/₄ hours.

As the months slip by, spring flowers peep through the damp soil, and as the primroses and violets sit in their clumps on banks and ditches, we think of Mothering Sunday.

> *I'll to thee a Simnel bring,*
> *Gainst thou go a'Mothering,*
> *So that when blesseth thee,*
> *Half that blessing thoul't bring me.*

Mid-Lent Sunday was originally when people went to visit their Mother Church, and so this was called Mothering Sunday. This was a great day for young girls, who had been put into service, living away from home. The mistress of the house would give the young girls a half a day off to go and visit their mother. What a treat this must have been for the young girls, as they would have only been about 12 - 14 years old. When the religious festival was forgotten, the Mid-Lent tradition of home visiting was continued. It had almost completely died out by the beginning of this century, but then the American influence of Mothering Sunday was revived in the fifties. As the girls walked many miles to see their mothers, they would stop and pick primroses and violets on the way.

Most of our churches still give out little posies and how nice to see the smiling faces go up to the alter to collect them, even if it's only 2 or 3 flowers with a piece of greenery. (Even nicer if its Rosemary, as this is taken as a token of Remembrance).

When I was a Sunday School teacher at St. Peter's Church, I have spent many a Saturday evening making up small posies of aconites, snowdrops and a few primroses, tied up in ivy leaves.

I must not forget to mention other presents the girls would take to their mothers. Most important a Simnel Cake. The name Simnel comes from a Latin word Simila - meaning the fine wheaten flour of which such cakes are made. A popular and quite unreliable legend which I was once told, was "a man named Simon and his wife Nell quarrelled at some unknown date about the cooking of a cake. One said the mixture should be boiled and the other that it should be baked. In the end the cake was boiled and baked, and the resulting confection was named Simnel, after both cooks. I don't know if this is true, but it's a nice little tale.

Sarah & Russell making biscuits and then licking the bowl out.

Patrick Anthony visited and made Akenfield Cake in my kitchen.

Simnel Cake

Sometimes this cake is made at Easter also. If you do make it, don't forget to put eleven almond paste balls for the topping to represent the Apostles, Judas not being included. Or you can use twelve almond balls to represent the months of the year. With a Mothering Sunday cake, just decorate with a few crystallised flowers, or a few sweetmeat eggs, which would look very dainty.

You will need the following ingredients:-

6 ozs butter or margarine
6 ozs soft brown sugar
3 large eggs
10 ozs SR flour
Pinch of salt
$^1/_2$ teaspoon mixed spice
5 - 6 tablespoons milk
2 teaspoons golden syrup (put spoon in hot water first and the syrup will run off easily)
1lb sultanas
6 ozs currants and raisins mixed
2 ozs glacé cherries (quartered)
4 ozs mixed peel
A little apricot jam
1lb almond paste

Method

Beat the butter and sugar together until light and fluffy, add the beaten eggs, one at a time, with a little flour, beating well after each addition. Stir in the salt and spice, add the milk and syrup with a little more flour. Fold in the remaining flour and the fruit and peel. Place half the mixture into a greased and lined 8 inch round cake tin and smooth level. Divide almond paste into two, roll out one piece to just under the size of your cake tin and place on top of the cake mixture. Cover with the remaining cake mixture. Bake in oven 350°F/180°C, Gas Mark 4 for one hour, then reduce the oven temperature to 275°F/140°C, Gas Mark 1, for a further $2^{1/2}$ hours.

Allow cake to cool, then divide the remaining almond paste for top of the cake. Brush with jam and place the rolled marzipan to fit cake. Don't forget to keep *a small* part of the paste for the little almond balls to place on the cake. You can stand on tin and put under the grill to brown top very lightly, this gives it a nice decorative finish.

❧

As I am still thinking about Easter when friends and families get together for meals. We often have a turkey, so this brings me to the stuffing used to stuff the turkey, and I am sure you will agree, what would we do if we could not have our "parsley". There is much country lore with this wonderful herb.

Parsley is one of the most difficult of herbs to grow, it was thought that it was best sown with curses on Good Friday, when you came home from Church; then you could be sure it came up, even so, it went nine times to the Devil and back again first !

You should add soot to the soil when you grow parsley. Sow parsley in April, July and February for a year round crop. Renew parsley beds every two years. I rather like this old saying, "The

Master of the House must quickly uproot over lush parsley in the garden, or he will have only girls born in the family".

Another saying is that "Parsley should only be sown by a woman, so that she flourishes like the parsley". But after all that, I will tell you, I sow my parsley in trays in the greenhouse, then prick it out into pots or the garden, it works well this way for me.

Another herb which I like is Angelica. You only have to brush past the large leaves and you get a sweet scent.

Angelica Stalks Crystallised

If you do them in early spring, choose young stems. April is the best time to do this. Cut into pieces about 3 - 4 inches long, boil until tender. Strip off outer skin, then return to the pan for a second boiling. The stems should look a nice green colour and ready for candying. I allow 1lb sugar to 1lb of Angelica stems. Place in a large bowl, coat with sugar, cover and leave for two days. Then boil well all together. Remove the Angelica, add 4 ozs sugar to the syrup and once more boil the Angelica in the syrup for about 10 minutes. Drain and dry in a cool oven, with the oven door slightly open. I store mine in a tight fitting jar. This method has been very useful for use on cake decorations and trifles etc. After having a morning cooking or even working in the garden, don't we all love our cup of tea. My first job when I wake up is to put my kettle on, it's the best cup of tea of the day. Sorry if you like coffee, but I like these few lines:-

> *Making a good cup of tea*
> *Be sure to heat the earthen pot*
> *And have your water boiling hot.*
> *Put in a teaspoonful per cup*

Taste of the Country Seasons

That each of you intend to sup.
Allow to stand for minutes four
Then off the leaves be sure to pour.
When serving, put the milk in first,
Add sugar and allay your thirst.
With this delightful fragrant brew,
You'll be refreshed and live anew.

A very old lady who was in service most of her life, sent me this little verse. I wonder what she would say to me with a mug and a tea bag and just pouring boiling water on it.

"A contented mind is a continual feast. "

At this time of the year it is nice to get the first fresh lettuce out of the greenhouse, and another salad green I like is watercress. When we were children we knew the best places to find it. The water was so clear in the streams in days gone by, where watercress used to flourish in abundance. Maybe you are one of the lucky ones and have a stream in your garden, where this bright gleaming green of flat leaves thrives. I know of a family who told me that their watercress is never out of season, and only a prolonged drought finishes the supply until it starts to grow again. My mother always had a bunch washed for our tea, and with homemade bread and farm butter it was very good. **Watercress spread** is good for a sandwich filling. All you need is chopped cress, a little lemon juice and some cottage cheese. Cut up the cress as though you were making mint sauce, add lemon juice and cheese. Mix until smooth.

Good for the diet

Eat watercress for a clear complexion. Rub the bruised leaves on your skin to help remove blemishes and spots.

Coloured eggs are traditional at Easter, as plum pudding is on Christmas Day 25th. Pretty objects to look at, if slightly dull to eat, but children love to see them, so here are some of my methods by which they can be made still more attractive.

First you gather leaves, grasses, and ferns, choosing those which have a pretty shape. Then fasten these individual bits and pieces of greenery on to the eggs, binding them securely in place with cotton thread. The eggs are subsequently dyed in the usual manner, with the brightest colours available. Afterwards they should be placed on a piece of paper to drain. When they are dry, cut the binding threads and the shapes of the leaves, you will be surprised what colours and shapes you get on your eggs!

Another nice vegetable which a good cottage garden should be able to grow, and if the pigeons have not eaten your plants over the winter months, is the cauliflower.

Try **cauliflower soufflé**:-

Ingredients

$1/2$oz butter
2 tomatoes skinned and sliced
1 cauliflower cooked and divided into florets
3 eggs
1 tablespoon milk
2 ozs grated cheese
$1/2$ teaspoon dry mustard
Salt and pepper to taste

Method

Melt the butter in a saucepan and add the tomatoes and cauliflower. Cook gently for five minutes. Meanwhile beat the egg yolks with the milk and 1 oz of the cheese, add the mustard and seasoning. Whisk the egg whites until stiff and fold into the yolk mixture. Turn the cauliflower mixture into a greased souffle dish and sprinkle over the remaining cheese. Spoon the egg mixture on top. Bake in a preheated oven 375°F/190°C or Gas Mark 5 for 20-30 minutes. Serve immediately.

This is something of a special dish, if you have friends to supper. If you don't want to go to the trouble of making a souffle, you can always fall back on **cauliflower cheese**. Just cook the vegetable, place in a greased dish, make a good cheese sauce, pour over the cauliflower and put under the grill for 5 - 10 minutes, or bake in a hot oven for the same time.

Good Friday is the day when many of us will be eating fish, and one of my favourite dishes is **fish pie**. First, a few facts about fish. White fish is nourishing - 17 per cent protein without being fattening (it's all the little extras that you put with the fish when cooking, which makes the calories go up). One can also cook it so lightly and it's so digestible and makes one of the best foods for tiny children or invalids.

General speaking you need just enough liquid to cover the fish, but remember if you boil rather than poach the fish, it will break up and become watery. Poach it in the oven or a frying pan, but be sure to grease whatever you cook it in to prevent fish sticking to it.

My Fish Pie

Ingredients

1 lb cod or haddock (in fact any white fish will do)
2 ozs butter
1 tablespoon plain flour
3 hard boiled eggs
4 ozs peeled shrimps or prawns
1 1/2 lb mashed potatoes
2 dessertspoons chopped parsley
1/2 pint milk
Salt and pepper

Method

Poach the fish until just tender and flake into large pieces. Reserve the cooking liquid. Melt butter, stir in flour and cook for one minute, then gradually add the milk and 1/2 pint stock. Cook until thick and smooth and season well. Add the chopped parsley.

Put a little sauce into the base of a fireproof dish, add a layer of fish, slice the eggs and put layers of egg, shrimps or prawns and continue until you have used up all the sauce, eggs and shrimps and fish. Top with mashed potatoes. Bake at 350°F/180°C or gas mark 4 for 30 minutes until crisp.

When cooking fish it leaves a smell around the house, try boiling a small stick of cinnamon for five minutes.

MICROWAVE OVENS

If anyone had told me a few years ago that I would enjoy working with a microwave oven, I just wouldn't have believed them, but after a short time I soon found how useful they are in any kitchen. I can't say I do my weekly baking in it, but it's so handy for putting a meal in when you want to heat it up. Also, it is useful for smaller jobs like cooking vegetables. Steam puddings are always a family favourite and this recipe takes only a fraction of the conventional steaming time, but remember, always use a larger pudding basin than you would normally use, as the microwave ovens tend to make puddings rise higher than usual.

Coffee Pudding with Chocolate Hazelnut Sauce
(cooking time 5 minutes plus standing time)

Ingredients

6ozs soft margarine
4 ozs soft brown sugar
6 ozs SR wholemeal flour
1 teaspoon baking powder
2 tablespoons coffee essence
3 eggs
2 ozs chopped hazelnuts
2 good tablespoons chocolate hazelnut spread

Method

Lightly grease a large pudding basin (3 pint size). In a mixing bowl place the margarine, sugar, flour, baking powder, coffee essence and eggs. Beat well with electric whisk until thoroughly blended. Spoon the chocolate and hazelnut spread onto the bottom of the basin and spoon the pudding mixture over the top. Level top of mixture with the back of a spoon, cover with a piece of cling film and pierce several holes in the top. Microwave at 100 (high) for five minutes, leave to stand for two minutes, then turn out. Sprinkle with hazelnuts and serve hot.

Some Do's and Don'ts for successful microwave cooking

DO remember to pierce items such as kidneys, liver or whole potatoes in skins when cooking in the microwave. If you don't they may explode.

DO cover or wrap food, either with a plate, cling film or roasting bags. This keeps the oven clean, and speeds up cooking time.

NB : If PVC cling film is used, do not allow it to touch food.

DO use the right size dish or plate as advised. Round, shallow ones are generally best for even heating.

DO let food stand where stated in the recipe. This is important for items such as cakes, fish and meats, which need to be left to stand to even up the cooking.

DO wipe up any spills immediately. Spilt food will continue to absorb energy and slow down cooking.

DON'T boil eggs in their shells in the microwave. It is not only impractical, but can also be dangerous, as they may explode.

DON'T thaw foods in one piece. Where possible, separate items such as sausages, fish cakes, etc. This will help speed up thawing time and help them to thaw evenly.

DON'T immerse vegetables in water. Potatoes, carrots and the like require only maximum depth of 3/4 inches (2 cm) in a shallow dish.

DON'T stir items cooked on a browning dish with a metal spoon. Use either plastic or wooden.

DON'T use any metallic bakeware or china rimmed with metal paint as this may cause damage to the microwave oven - an expensive mistake!

❦

Banana Slice

This is a good cake to make if you get some cheap ripe bananas. Its quick to make and keeps well.

Ingredients:-

8 ozs S.R. floor
A good pinch of salt
$1/2$ teaspoon mixed spice
4 ozs margarine
4 ozs caster sugar
1 tablespoon honey
4 ozs sultanas
2 ozs glacé cherries (quartered)
3 ozs walnuts (chopped)
1lb mashed bananas
2 beaten eggs

Method

Grease a 2lb loaf tin. Sift flour, salt and spice in a bowl. Add margarine, cut into pieces, add all remaining ingredients and beat well with a wooden spoon until the mixture is well blended and smooth. Put into loaf tin and bake in centre of oven 350°F/180°C or Gas No. 4 for about 1 hour, then reduce heat to 300°F/150°C, Gas 2 1/2 for a further 30 minutes, or until testing skewer comes out clean. Cool on wire tray.

The following verse was given to me by a visitor to my garden. I think it is interesting and so true in many of the lines.

Always have lobster sauce with salmon
And put mint sauce with roasted lamb on.
Veal cutlets, dip in egg and breadcrumbs,
Fry until you see a brownish red come.
Grate Gruyere cheese on macaroni,
Make the top crisp, but not too bony.
Roast pork sans apple sauce past doubt,
Is "Hamlet" with the "Prince" left out.
Boiled turkey, gormets know, of course,
Is exquisite with celery sauce.
The cook deserves a hearty cuffing
Who serves roast fowl with tasteless stuffing.
Egg sauce, few make it right alas,
Is good with bluefish or white bass.
Buy plump-fed pigeons, when you've got them
The way to cook them, is to pot them.
Roast veal with rich stock gravy serve
And redcurrant jelly to observe.

Mixed Nut Pudding

Always after Christmas there seems to be a lot of nuts hanging around. I get my brother to have a night or two cracking all the left-over nuts. Some I put into cakes (Date & Walnut). Flapjacks, I put chopped walnuts in and Chestnuts I use for soup. But the following recipe I made up as if I was making bread and butter pudding without the bread.

Take and grease a 2 pint oven proof dish. Mix in a bowl 6 ozs sugar, 4 large eggs, then whisk until creamy and thick. Fold in 8 ozs chopped mixed nuts, filberts or cob nuts, walnuts and a few almonds, (I usually put all the nuts in my food processor). Add a good pinch of nutmeg. Turn into a greased dish and bake at about 350°F/180°C or Gas No. 4 until set. It's nice hot or cold.

Joan's Scalloped Potato Dish

When I went to America, Joan made me a super dish.
She had a 3 - 4 pint fireproof dish greased with layers of potatoes (2lbs) thinly sliced. A small onion, also thinly sliced, about 3/4 pint of milk. Salt and pepper and flour. 3 ozs butter or margarine and 6 ozs cheddar cheese grated.

First put in the dish a layer of potatoes and onions, then knobs of margarine or butter, sprinkle with flour, carry on until all the potatoes and onions are used up. Add salt and pepper, then add grated cheese on top. Bake in oven for $1^1/2$ hours at 375°F/190°C or Gas 5.
You can always put some leftover ham or sausages in with the potatoes to make a mixed dish.

My Country Flan

There is something I like very much about the month of April. I suppose really because birds are singing from early morning, spring flowers are coming out in full colours, and it just makes you feel good to see the start of new growth.

As I get busy in my greenhouse at this time of the year I like to make a few meals to put in my freezer, so if I am rather tired, I can just get a meal out. What luxury! What would we do without freezers. I find savoury flans or the posh word "quiche", a good standby which freezes well.

Some people bake blind pastry, but I line my dishes with pastry and then put the following ingredients in and make altogether. (This recipe makes two flans).

Ingredients

1/2 pint milk
4 large eggs
10 ozs cheese (grated)
Good pinch of salt and pepper

Method

Mix altogether in a bowl. Then take 6 rashers of bacon and 2 onions. Fry chopped onions and bacon in a little fat or oil. Put the bacon and onion into the pastry cases, next pour on the egg and cheese mixture. Slice three tomatoes, and if you have any spare mushrooms, put some slices in the mixture with a little chopped parsley. Bake at 350°F/180°C or Gas Mark 4 for 1/2 to 3/4 hour.

Bean and Cabbage Salad

A nice salad goes well with savoury flans. Try this one. I was given this salad with steak when I was lecturing in the USA. The American ladies made some wonderful meals for me when I was going from State to State, and the salads stayed in my memory for a long time.

Ingredients

1/2lb shredded cabbage
1/2lb stick diced celery
4 small chopped onions or shallots
(if you have them)
1 397 gram can of kidney beans (drained)
1 tablespoon vinegar
4 ozs mayonnaise
Salt and pepper to taste
2 tablespoons chopped parsley

Method

Mix beans, cabbage, celery, parsley and shallots together and toss. Stir vinegar into mayonnaise, give a shake with pepper and salt. Pour over salad mixture. Serve in lettuce lined salad bowl.

In Ohio I first saw spinach used as a salad vegetable.

Spinach Salad

Ingredients

1lb fresh spinach
1 397 gram packet or can bean sprouts
$1/2$lb cooked bacon rashers (cooked nice and crisp)
4 hard boiled eggs
1 medium sized sliced onion (red if you can get one)

For the dressing

8 fl. ozs oil
4 fl. ozs red wine vinegar
4ozs sugar
3 fl. ozs ketchup
1 teaspoon salt (optional)

Method

Mix together in a jar with a tight lid. Chill. Shake occasionally until needed. This will keep for weeks in the fridge.

Round about this time of the year I start to get bookings to go and judge at the local flower shows. These shows are still big events in the villages, and you would be surprised to see the wonderful cake and pastries which are entered. The following recipe is for Cobblestone Cake. It was very popular at the Spring Show held in a nearby horticultural college.

Cobblestone Cake
(Makes one 2lb fruit loaf)

Ingredients

6 ozs soft margarine
6 ozs castor sugar
3 eggs
4 ozs sultanas
3 ozs glacé cherries (chopped)
1 oz Angelica (chopped)
8 ozs plain flour
$1/2$ level teaspoon baking powder

Topping

2 ozs glacé cherries halved
3 tablespoons apricot jam

Method

Grease a 2lb loaf tin and line it with greased greaseproof paper. Place the margarine, sugar, eggs, sultanas, glacé cherries and angelica in a mixing bowl. Sift the flour and baking powder into the bowl. Beat together with a wooden spoon for 3-4 minutes until well blended. Spoon the mixture into prepared tin. Smooth the top and place the halved cherries in rows along the top and bake in a moderately slow oven at 325°F/170°C or Gas Mark 3 for $1^{1/2}$ - $1^{3/4}$ hours. Turn cake out of the tin onto wire rack to cool. Heat the apricot jam in saucepan and when boiled, sieve it. Brush jam over the cake.

As the new green growth comes to our country fields, the farmers start to worry as the fields of oil seed rape get attacked by the pigeons. The birds simply love to eat the new green shoots, so at weekends the farmers have shooting parties to kill off some of the birds, as they do so much damage. Pigeons are cheap food and make some delicious meals, but they do need slow cooking to get the best out of them. You will need 2 - 3 birds to make a good meal. Some people pluck the pigeons, but I just cut the breasts off, as by the time you have plucked the whole bird you don't get much more meat, only on the breasts (but that's just my views).

Pigeon Casserole

Ingredients

Breasts of 2 - 3 pigeons
4 streaky rashers of bacon
2 ozs dripping
1 large onion sliced
1 tablespoon flour seasoned with salt and pepper
Enough water to cover ingredients
(I use 1/2 pint homemade wine)
4 ozs mushrooms
1 beef stock cube

Method

Fry the bacon in the dripping and place on bottom of casserole. Fry onions and add to the bacon. Dip the pigeon breasts into seasoned flour and fry lightly on both sides until they are browned. Lay the breasts on bacon and onion, then mix the remaining flour with water or homemade wine, add crumbled stock cube, stir until you get a creamy sauce mixture and pour over the birds. Cover and cook slowly for 2 - 3 hours at 325°F/170°C or Gas Mark 3. You can put potatoes in the oven to bake at the same time to serve with the casserole. By the way, I cook my rabbits in the same way. The slower the cooking, I find, the better.

My mother used to make **pigeon pudding** by just lining a pudding basin with a suet pastry, she then put the pigeon breasts onto the pastry with sliced onion and bacon. Then she filled up the basin with stock (water and a beef cube) almost to the top and put on a lid of suet pastry, tied down the pudding basin with a cloth and put basin in a saucepan, filled half way up with water, brought it to the boil and let it simmer for 3 - 4 hours.

Years ago meat puddings would have been made first thing in the morning, then this pudding would have cooked on the cooking range all the morning, nice and slow. These puddings were delicious, maybe rather fattening, but it was good wholesome food.

One of the best places to buy homemade cakes, pastries and biscuits is the Women's Institute Markets. Over the years they have become very popular and can arrange a hamper of home cooked food from one end of the country to another in the British Isles. I have met many good cooks, and each week I take preserves, fruit and vegetables, and plants when in season, to my local W.I. market in Woodbridge. We often take and discuss recipes with each other, and one lady I got to know was Wilma Kelley, who used to cook for the Woodbridge W.I. Market. When she left to return to her home in the USA, she gave me her **Pineapple Carrot Cake** recipe, and here it is:-

Ingredients

$1/2$lb plain flour
$1/2$ lb sugar
2 teaspoons baking powder
$1^1/2$ teaspoon bicarbonate of soda
1 teaspoon salt
2 teaspoons cinnamon
3 eggs
12fl. ozs oil
$1/2$lb carrots
10 ozs crushed pineapple
1 oz chopped nuts

Method

Preheat oven to 350°F/180°C or Gas Mark 4. Grease 2 large flan tins and dust with flour. In a large bowl mix flour, sugar, baking powder, bicarbonate of soda, salt and cinnamon. Stir in eggs and oil until well blended. Add grated carrots, pineapple and nuts. Divide into flan tins or dishes, filling each just about half full. Bake for 25 - 30 minutes. Cool before icing.

For the Icing

8 ozs cream cheese
4 ozs butter
8 ozs icing sugar
1 teaspoon vanilla extract

Have cheese and butter very soft and beat everything together until smooth and fluffy. Spread lightly over the cakes. if icing seems too thick to spread, just add a few drops of milk.

❧

Recipes for Market Bargains

I am sure that many housewives love a bargain, and on the fruit and vegetable stalls, at the end of the day, you can buy fruit and vegetables very cheap, as the traders don't want to take a lot of their produce back home.

When I look around these markets, I am looking for fruit for wine making. Sometimes I can buy a whole case of grapes, peaches or bananas. They may be a little bruised or the banana skins maybe black, but don't be put off, as you can make lovely Banana Wine and cakes. The fruit is fine underneath the skins.

Banana & Walnut Cake

You will find a good flavour with this cake, and it also freezes well.

Ingredients

3 ozs butter
6 ozs castor sugar
2 small eggs beaten
3 bananas
8 ozs plain flour
1 teaspoon bicarbonate of soda

1 teaspoon baking powder
1/2 teaspoon grated nutmeg
2 tablespoons milk
2 ozs chopped walnuts

Method

Set the oven to 350°F/180°C or Gas Mark 4. Grease and line a 9 inch cake tin. Beat the butter and sugar together until light and creamy, add eggs gradually and beat well between each addition. Mash the bananas and beat into the mixture a spoonful at a time. Fold in the sifted flour, bicarbonate of soda, baking powder and nutmeg. Stir in the milk and walnuts and pour mixture into the cake tin. Bake for $1^1/4$ - $1^1/2$ hours. As soon as the cake looks set, remove it from the oven and turn out on to a wire rack.

At this time of the year housewives start to sort out the freezers and use up soft fruit etc. I often get a surprise and have forgotten fruit or meat which I had put in the freezer six months ago. If I find apple slices I may make a sweet called Apple Charlotte. My mother used to make this a lot for us children. It was cheap and a good way to use up stale bread.

Apple Charlotte

Ingredients

6 slices of buttered bread
$1^1/2$lb cooking apples
A little grated nutmeg
$1/4$ pint water

In addition, you will need 2 tablespoons golden syrup, or you can use black treacle and 2 tablespoons soft brown sugar

Method

Butter an ovenproof dish and line the bottom and sides with the buttered slices of bread. Put sliced apples in a dish, when you have filled it, grate over a little nutmeg. Pour over the water and syrup and sprinkle with half the sugar, then top up with more slices of bread, butter side up. Sprinkle over the rest of sugar and bake in oven 350°F/180°C or gas mark 4. Serve hot with cream!!

❧

As the sun gets a little more stronger, we seem to spend more time outside, and often turn to come indoors to get a cool drink. The hedgerows are full of free blossom for making drinks. Broom or gorse make a delicious wine, also bramble tips, oak leaf and May blossom. But I will go into wine making later on in this book. However, one drink which is so easy to make is Elderflower Champagne, and I will give you this recipe now.

Elderflower Champagne

It's a nice cooling drink, but be careful to pick the flowers when they are just out and not falling, otherwise it will make the champagne bitter.

Take 8 - 10 heads of elderflowers
1 lemon
1¹/₂lbs white sugar

2 tablespoons white wine vinegar
1 gallon of cold water

Method

Pick the heads when in full bloom. Take off any green stems, however small. Put the blossoms into a bowl and sprinkle over the juice of lemon. Grate the rind and add this along with the sugar and vinegar. Add the cold water and leave for 24 hours. Strain into bottles and cork firmly. Do not disturb for two weeks, when the champagne should be sparkling and ready to drink. This champagne should last up to three months.

Elderflower Cordial
(easy to make)

Take 4 oranges
4 lemons
3lbs sugar
2 ozs tartaric acid
10 heads of Elderflowers (no more no less)
4 pints boiled water, then cooled

Method

Just slice the oranges and lemons. Dissolving the sugar in the water (while still warm). Pour this, with the fruit slices, over the Elderflower heads, adding tartaric acid. Cover and leave for two days. Stirring two or three times a day, then strain and bottle. Dilute to taste.

Summer

Elderflowers have a powerful smell. If you use too many in recipes you get the smell of, dare I say it, cat's pee! On the other hand, a few flower heads will improve gooseberries when cooking.

SUMMER - VEGETABLES

By early summer it is a difficult time for vegetables. The broccoli and purple sprouting are nearly finished. I always feel white and purple sprouting broccoli are one of the nicest vegetables, but so many people spoil it by over cooking. I like it served on its own with a cheese sauce.

Autumn broad beans will soon be fit; they are another vegetable where people just eat the beans from the pods, but did you know, you can eat the whole pods while small, also the tops of the plant can be pinched out and eaten as spinach.

Asparagus is another vegetable which needs to be eaten young to bring out the delicate flavour. New potatoes are now available and how good they taste, but the best ones are from our gardens. There is no need to peel or scrape them because much of the flavour lies just under the skin. There are many new varieties coming out each year, but one called "Fir Apple" is very good for salads. It's a long knobbly tuber with a fine flavour and has a waxy texture.

Herb & Vegetable Remedies

There are so many old wives tales about giving good advice with herbs and vegetables. Some folk swear by chewing a raw onion, and indeed there is plenty of evidence that onions and their first cousins garlic, are good for the common cold. Nothing is more nourishing and comforting than a hot baked onion. My father used to love onion gruel, when he had a cold coming on. Onions boiled in a little milk with a little margarine or butter, salt and pepper to taste, and eaten as hot as possible, helps to stave off the onset of a cold.

If you find that the smell of onion or garlic lies unpleasantly on your breath, you can always chew a few sprigs of parsley, picked fresh from the garden. Parsley is brimful of vitamin C and will absorb all the unpleasant odours of the onion family.

Mixtures of honey and lemon are very comforting. To enjoy the full benefit of this remedy, try spiking a hole in the top of a lemon and filing it with clear honey. Stand the lemon in a small tinfoil container and bake in a moderate oven for ten minutes. Pour out the juices and you will have a soothing syrup for sore throats and hacking coughs.

Cough Treatments

Ingredients

2 tablespoons dried peppermint leaves
2 tablespoons thyme leaves
2 tablespoons sage leaves
2 pints boiling water

Method

Put all the herbs into a large jug, pour on the boiling water and cover with a small plate. Leave for five minutes to infuse.

To use - sit in a comfortable chair with the jug on your knees. Cover yourself and the jug with a large bath towel, breath gently for about ten minutes and you will find yourself surrounded with a healing aroma which is a great help in relieving catarrhal problems.

Hot Drinks for Colds

Ingredients

1 garlic clove crushed
Juice of one lemon
$1/2$ teaspoon ground ginger
Pinch of cayenne pepper
1 tablespoon honey
1 teacup boiling water

Method

Put all the ingredients into a warmed earthenware or china cup. Pour in the boiling water and leave covered with a saucer for ten minutes. Drink the liquid as soon as possible.

Some old mint remedies

Hang a bunch of mint in the kitchen to keep the flies away in the summer. Try to have a jug of mint and marigolds on your kitchen table, this will help to absorb the cooking smells.

When sheep shearing was one of the annual festivals, men washed their hands in the water in which wild mint had been added, to cut the grease and eliminate the smell.

The oil of peppermint is said to be one of the best, safest and most agreeable of all antiseptics. When applied to the temples it will help to relieve a headache, and when rubbed into the gums will relieve toothache. Peppermint water relieves indigestion and will take away the feeling of sickness or nausea when at sea.

This is made by pouring a pint of boiling water on the fresh tops of peppermint leaves and taking a small quantity when necessary.

A Mint Alternative

You may not always wish to serve mint sauce. As an alternative, try this jelly recipe:-

Gooseberry & Mint Jelly

Ingredients

3lbs gooseberries
Water to cover
1 tablespoon white wine vinegar
Sugar
Mint

Method

Top, tail and wash gooseberries. Put them into a pan and add water and vinegar, simmer until fruit is very soft. Add one pound of sugar to each pint of juice, and suspend a bunch of washed mint in the pan. Stir until sugar has dissolved. Increase the heat and boil until setting point is reached, tasting from time to time, and removing the mint when the flavour is strong enough.

Rosemary is another rewarding herb. In earlier years it was thought that where rosemary flourished the woman ruled. It is also known as the herb for remembrance and friendship. This evergreen aromatic herb is also one of the oldest medicinal plants. When drinking Rosemary as an infusion, it stimulates the circulation and helps low blood pressure. When my late husband used to dig graves in the village churchyard, he once had a request to line a grave out with sprays of Rosemary. The following lines made me think of this:-

Grow it for two ends, it matters not at all
Be't for my bridal or my burial

(Robert Herrick)

Rosemary is most often associated with lamb, but pork, beef and poultry all benefit from a hint of rosemary. I often put a few sprigs in my stews. Basil is another herb which I like. It's a true herb of the sun, a perfect accompaniment for tomatoes and other summer vegetables. A mere pinch sprinkled over a tomato salad will work magic. To preserve the flavour for winter salads, steep the leaves in a bottle of white wine vinegar.

Bay trees are often in pots and tubs, and often seen standing outside houses and restaurants. A wonderful herb where leaves can be gathered all year round and used dry or fresh.

The bay leaf is an essential part of a "bouquet garni". I often pop outside to pick fresh leaves off my bay tree when I make white sauces and sweet rice puddings, and it gives a piquant flavour to steaming fish.

Sage officinalis is an old fashioned semi-evergreen herb, hence the old proverb, 'Set sage in May and it will grow always'.

Throughout the world there are many different varieties of sage from the highly decorative garden plants with variegated leaves to the wild varieties. Many cooks prefer the narrow leaved white sage, and this is the one most commonly found in English and American gardens. Some people say the red sage officinalis purpunea has the finer flavour, while those who can obtain the wild variety may find it surpasses all others for its strong spicy flavour.

Since early times sage has been thought to aid in the digestion of rich meats. What would some of our English sausages be without some flavoured sage? This wonderful herb also has its medicinal uses, you would often hear the quote, "Why should a man die when sage grows in his garden".

Sage goes well with pork and it's also excellent with cheese in cooked dishes. Sage tea is a pleasant and refreshing drink. An old Welsh lore suggests that a sage gargle should be used in all dangerous seasons, when epidemic sore throats prevail, this, with God's blessing, will preserve you.

Herbs, Oils & Vinegars

Take a small bunch of fresh herbs, say, three or four sprigs, and put into a bottle of olive oil or wine vinegar, it will give a wonderful fragrance, also add a pinch of sea salt, more if it's a strong herb, such as Rosemary or Peppercorn. Give the oil or vinegar a few weeks to absorb the flavour before using it.

Preserving Herbs

Herbs should be picked just before they flower. Choose a fine morning, cut long steins and tie them loosely in small bunches. Then leave them in a cool dark place to dry naturally. Avoid artificial heat, and keep different herbs separate or the flavours will blend.

When herbs are dry, rub between your palms the brittle leaves off the stalks and store them in tightly fitted dark glass jars.

The flavour of dried herbs is much stronger than that of fresh herbs. One teaspoonful of dried herbs equals approximately three teaspoonfuls of chopped fresh ones.

Freezing Herbs

Deep freezing is the most successful method of retaining the natural flavour of herbs. To prepare them for freezing, cut the herbs, with their stems left on, then dip them carefully into boiling water to set the colour. Pat them dry and deep freeze. Spread out loosely in well-sealed plastic envelopes. Another method is to chop the herbs finely and pack them tightly into individual ice-cube trays, cover with water and freeze. Put the frozen cubes in a plastic bag for storage in the freezer.

Edible Flowers

While I am writing about herbs, my mind goes on to think about eating flowers, and using them in salads, etc. Nasturtium flowers, leaves and seeds can be eaten. The seeds make super capers when pickled in vinegar. Rose petals make jam. Lime blossom and hawthorn can also be eaten. Courgette flowers make a delicious dish if fried, or you can even use hollyhock flowers if you have no courgettes.

CHEESE RECIPES

My mother used to say, if you have only bread and cheese in the house, then you can always have a meal.

Since the days of her cooking, there are a lot more cheeses around. Denmark must be the place to see cheese, as it's one of the largest exporters of dairy products in the world. They make hard cheese, semi soft cheese and blue and white mould cheeses. One only has to look at old photographs and read what the farmworker lived on in the fields, mainly bread and cheese. I can remember one old man who used to work on the roads, and his lunch every day would be bread and cheese wrapped in newspaper. He would cut off a lump of cheese, bit by bit, making it last as long as the bread. It was a picture to watch him.

Stilton must be England's prize cheese, so try:-

Stilton Dip

Ingredients

8 ozs Stilton cheese
4 ozs cream cheese
4 tablespoons milk
4 finely chopped pickled onions

Method

Cream cheeses until well blended. Beat in milk and stir chopped pickled onions into cheese mixture. Season with salt and pepper and serve with a crusty brown bread.

Cheese Scotch Eggs

Ingredients

6ozs cheddar cheese
1¹/₂ ozs plain flour
1 level teaspoon salt
1 level teaspoon Worcester sauce
1 large egg beaten
1- 2 tablespoons milk
4 large hardboiled eggs
1¹/₂ ozs fresh white breadcrumbs
Deep fat for frying

Method

Grate cheese and mix with flour, salt and Worcester sauce. Add beaten egg and milk, mix well. Using wet hands, coat the hardboiled eggs completely with the cheese mixture. Roll in the breadcrumbs. Heat fat in deep fryer. Fry eggs for 1-2 minutes, or until golden brown and the mixture is cooked throughout. Drain on kitchen paper.

Cheese cakes or scones, even cheese rusks were always put in father's work lunch box. Cheese cakes in days gone by were not like the sweet of today called "Cheese Cake".

My **Cheese Cakes** are like scones and this is how you make them:-

Ingredients

1lb SR flour
^{1}/$_2$ teaspoon salt
1 level teaspoon mustard
2 ozs butter or margarine
8 ozs good strong grated cheese
2 beaten eggs
A little milk

Method

Sift flour, salt and mustard into a mixing bowl, rub in the butter and add 7 ozs cheese. Bind together with eggs (and milk if needed) to form a soft dough. Roll out onto a floured board to ^{1}/$_2$ inch in thickness and cut into rounds, using a 1^1/$_2$ inch plain round cutter. Place rounds on a baking sheet, brush with milk and sprinkle over the remaining cheese. Bake in preheated hot oven for 15 minutes. Serve cold, sliced in half and sandwiched with butter and cheese.

A tip - if you make scones for a village or County show, fruit scones should be cut out with a pretty shaped cutter, but savoury scones must be cut out with a plain round cutter.

Suffolk Rusks are a delicious compliment to cheese.

Ingredients

1lb S.R. flour
A good pinch of salt
6 ozs fat (3ozs lard, 3 ozs margarine)
2 eggs and a little water to mix

Method

Rub the fats into the flour and salt, then with the beaten eggs mix to a smooth dough. Roll out to 1 inch thickness and cut into rounds - about $2^{1/2}$ inch - and bake at 450°F for about 10 - 12 minutes. Remove from the oven, and cut open, then return to the oven for a further 10 - 15 minutes or until a nice golden brown. When cold these rusks are delicious eaten with a bit of butter or cheese.

Peggy, with a selection of baking, preserves and wine

Evelyn & Peggy at work on material for the book

Soft Fruit

The soft fruit season has come around once more. I am lucky, as I live surrounded by fields in my area where you can pick your own fruit. There is a local farmer in my village who has many orchards of wonderful fruit. But times have changed since I first married. I can remember the season started with gooseberry picking, which lasted two weeks or more, then it was the blackcurrant season, which went on for nearly three weeks. I can see mothers now starting off in the mornings, walking with young babies in prams with food for the day. Children used to rush from school to get up to the fields to help mum pick the currants. It was hard earned money, but they enjoyed the fresh air and many stopped in the fields until eight o'clock at night. This has now all stopped and a large machine comes into the fields, cuts the bushes and gathers the fruit at the same time, so now we go and buy our blackcurrants all ready picked. Village life has changed so much in the last twenty years. (I keep telling my friend Ronald Blythe, who based his book *Akenfield*, on village life and nearby villages, that he should update the changes that have taken place in village life). Women still go to work in the orchards, but not so many and they arrive at the fields in cars, not walking or cycling. They do most of the tree pruning then start picking plums, apples and pears. I do wonder how long this will last as fruit is produced from overseas at a much cheaper rate. Now the farmers are being paid money to pull out our wonderful orchards. I do hope we don't lose our Cox and Bramley apples.

Now I must give you some recipes for fruit puddings. I am always amazed at the sweets which turn up at our village for open suppers and barbecues. Pavlovas are always the first pudding to go.

Pavlova

Ingredients

4 egg whites
8 ozs castor sugar
1 teaspoon cornflour
1 teaspoon vinegar
1 teaspoon vanilla essence
Greaseproof paper

Method

Whisk egg whites until they form stiff peaks, add sugar, a little at a time, then stir in cornflour. Add vanilla essence and vinegar and whisk together. Then place on a greased baking tray, lined with greaseproof paper, forming a circle of about 8 inches in diameter. Bake for about 1 hour at 250°F/120°C or gas mark $^1/_2$.

For the filling

Ingredients

$^1/_2$ pint double cream or whipping cream
Any soft fruits, such as strawberries or raspberries, etc.

When Pavlova is cooked, fill with cream and top with fresh fruits. I sprinkle a little lemon juice to prevent discolouration.

Plum & Marshmallow Pie

Ingredients

8 ozs S.R. flour
Pinch of salt
6 ozs margarine & lard mixed (or cooking fat)
1 large egg
1¹/₂lb plums
4 ozs marshmallows
4 ozs demerara sugar
Icing sugar

Method

Mix fat and salt in mixing bowl with flour until mixture resembles fine bread crumbs. Separate the egg and lightly beat the yolk with a fork and add this to pastry mixture. You may need a little extra milk to make mixture into a stiff ball. Roll out ³/4 of the pastry and line pie dish. (Keep remaining ¹/4 pastry). Stone the plums and halve the marshmallows. Arrange the plums and marshmallows in a 2 pint oval pie dish and sprinkle with the demerara sugar. With the rest of the pastry make a lid and put on top of the pie, making a hole in the lid. Stand the pie dish on a baking sheet and bake in the centre of a hot oven - 425°F/220°C or Gas No. 7 for 10 minutes, then reduce heat to 350°F/180°C or Gas No. 4 and cook for a further 30-40 minutes.

When cooked:-
With the egg white, beat in enough icing sugar to give a light coating and dribble the icing over the top of the baked pie with a

teaspoon, making lines across the top. Brown lightly and quickly under hot grill, no more than two minutes. Serve warm with cream - delicious.

My Quick Strawberry Cheesecake

Very often I am asked to make a sweet for some function or someone coming to lunch. This sweet doesn't need much cooking and I do try to have a spare sponge flan case by me. You can always make a batch of cases, then freeze them if you don't want to buy shop ones.

Ingredients

Take one 8 inch flan case, and for the filling - 3 tablespoons strawberry conserve or jam.
$1/2$ pint strawberry yoghurt
8 ozs cream cheese

Method

Cut and lay the strawberries on top of flan. Place flan case on dish and spoon in strawberry conserve, beat cream cheese until soft and smooth, then add yoghurt and mix well. Spoon mixture into flan case and chill for $1/2$ hour. Take out of fridge, cut a strawberry and lay on top of flan. Sometimes I will grate a little chocolate on top, or I keep a box of chocolate leaves in my store cupboard and they come in handy for decoration. Serve with thin cream.

I make another quick sweet with pears.

Gingered Pears

Ingredients

Take 6 large pears
$1/2$ pint cold water
2 ozs sugar
Juice of small lemon (or a few drops from a Jif lemon)
3 tablespoons ginger syrup from a jar of stem ginger
About 6 lumps of stem ginger,
cut up 9 - 10 ginger biscuits

Method

Peel and core pears. Place the water and sugar in a saucepan. Stir gently until the sugar has dissolved. Add the pears, cover and simmer slowly until tender. Add lemon juice and ginger syrup. Pour the pears and syrup into dish where biscuits and sliced ginger have been placed. Serve hot or cold with cream or chocolate ice cream.

When the first cooking apples are ready, it's nice to have fresh ones.

A recipe using apples on fish was given to me by Olive Cass MBE, who was Publicity Secretary to the Garden Horticultural Society at County Hall, London, SE1. Olive got to know me through one of her friends hearing me talk about gardening on our local radio station each week. She asked me to go to London and give a talk at their Club. I have never forgotten it, as it was such a large place and I did not know which door to go in - what a huge place it is. The President, Lord Birkett, met me and I had a most enjoyable evening talking and showing slides of my country ways. After that visit Olive used to send me their monthly news, *Gardening and Domestic Scene,* which is a most interesting magazine.

Fish & Apple Bake
(Serves 4)

Ingredients

1lb white fish
1¹/2 lbs cooking apples, sliced finely (I use Bramleys)
10 ozs soft bread crumbs
4 tablespoons chopped Parsley
Paprika pepper
4 ozs dripping or butter

Method

Cover the base of a well-greased oven proof dish with half the breadcrumbs. Divide the fish into 4 pieces and place on breadcrumbs. Arrange the apple and parsley on top, then sprinkle generously with Paprika pepper and the remainder of the breadcrumbs. Cover with foil and cook in a hot oven for 30 minutes. Remove foil and continue cooking for a further 5 - 10 minutes until top is crisp and golden brown.

Serve with peas and carrots tossed in butter, and if you are extra hungry, have a baked potato as well!

At this time of the year I just have to make time and go to Polstead in Suffolk. Polstead is well known in history where the Red Barn murder took place. Polstead is famous for growing cherries. At one time it had many orchards, but over the years this has declined. But in the past it was well known for growing sweet cherries and Morello cherries, which are sharper.

There is nothing like **Black Cherry Wine**.

Ingredients

5lbs Morello cherries
3lbs sugar
6 pints cold water
Pectin enzyme, campden tablet
Wine yeast and yeast nutrient

Method

Remove the stalks and stones from cherries. Wash fruit and place the cherries in a large bowl, crush fruit with plastic spoon. Pour on cold water, adding Campden tablet and pectin enzyme, wine yeast and yeast nutrient. Leave for a week keeping closely covered, but stir each day and mash the fruit with your hands. Strain through a muslin cloth. Do not squeeze or hurry process. Once the liquid has been strained add sugar. Leave for another 3 days, then put into fermenting bottle and fit airlock. Rack off into clean bottles and keep for six months (if you can!).

I always make **Cherry Brandy** with the same variety of cherries.

Ingredients

1lb Morello cherries
¹/₂lb castor sugar
1 bottle Vodka (lower strength) or you can use cheap brandy

Method

Stalk and wash fruit, drain dry and pierce each cherry several times (just like you do to sloes for Sloe Gin). Put fruit in large jar and sprinkle the sugar on in layers. Cover fruit with Vodka. Fix and cover jar. Shake the jar a little to ensure the dissolution of the sugar and store for 6 months or so. Strain off the liqueur, which is immediately ready for use. The cherries I put into trifles or sometimes into my gallon of cherry wine to give it an extra kick.

You can make damson liqueur, and peach and damson, using the same recipe.

I also drive down to Sudbourne near Orford and pick loganberries. I call this my treat, as I go early in the morning. Birds are singing and when you look out to the sea it's so peaceful. The loganberries are easy to pick, but you must remember to pick the black ones - the red ones are not ripe.

Recipe to make a gallon of **Loganberry Wine**:-

Ingredients

4lbs loganberries

3lbs sugar
6 pints water
Yeast, Campden tablet and nutrient

Method

Put berries in a bucket and cover with 6 pints boiling water and Campden tablet. Mash and leave covered for 3 days, stirring and mashing occasionally. Strain on to the sugar and stir, warm slightly and add yeast. Leave covered for 24 hours, then put into fermentation jar. When fermentation ceases, rack, mature and bottle.

I like to keep all my wines one year before drinking. Plus I keep wine in gallon jars for at least 6 months or longer before bottling - the reason - "it goes too quick".

Gooseberry wine is one of my favourites. It tastes like a good Hock.

Ingredients

5lbs fruit (ripe green gooseberries)
2³/4lb sugar
6 - 7 pints water
Yeast and nutrient, pectin and enzyme

Method

Top, tail and wash gooseberries. Put into a large bucket, try to squeeze by hand, add pectin, enzyme and water. Allow to stand for 4 days well covered. Strain, then add sugar, stirring until it is all dissolved, then add yeast and yeast nutrient. Put into fermenting bottle and fit air-lock. Leave to mature, siphoning off the lees after 6 months. Leave for one year if you can before drinking.

From the Rose

Summer can't be without roses. I love evenings, walking around my garden, the perfume is so strong, and I can understand why **rosewater** was known as early as 140 B.C It is used for many purposes, as a flavouring as well as for perfume, and a little rosewater mixed with glycerine makes a pleasant hand lotion. A teaspoonful in whipped cream is delicious with strawberries, and a teaspoonful, or more, gives a delicate flavour to sponge cakes or ice-cream. The deep scented red roses are the best, because they have a strong perfume and colour water a pale pink.

Fill a pan with red rose petals, remove any white heel because this has a bitter taste, cover petals with water and keep at boiling point, but do not boil. After an hour, remove petals and add fresh ones. Repeat until the desired strength has been reached. Strain and bottle.

Rose Vinegar

This is delicious in a fruit salad. Half fill a jar with rose petals, cover with best white wine vinegar and steep for 24 hours, preferably in the sun, then strain. A handkerchief dipped in rose vinegar is used by French women to allay a headache, as it's cool and refreshing. Candied or preserved rose petals can be used to decorate a cake or to place on top of whipped cream. Beat egg whites, but do not beat to too stiff a froth. Paint each rose petal on each side with egg white, using a clean paint brush or a pastry brush. Spread the petals on greaseproof paper and place on a baking tray, powder both sides with castor sugar. Dry in the sun or in a cool oven for an hour. When crisp and dry store in an airtight tin with tissue paper between the layers.

June is the month when the strawberries come into the shops in abundance. Their season is short and we have to make the most of these delicious fruits while we can. Dr. Butter, the 16th century physician, wrote, "Doubtless God could have made a better berry, but doubtless God never did". He was talking about the strawberry, the fruit which symbolizes perfection in an English summer garden, jewel red against its bright green cap.

Unless strawberries are very dirty, avoid washing them. If it is really necessary, simply put them in a colander, one layer at a time. Spray them with water and shake them dry.

Many of you will only consider serving strawberries with cream. They are just as delicious served in sweet white wine or covered with raspberry puree.

My Strawberry Tart

This tart can be made with other fruit such as raspberries or loganberries.

The pastry is a bit different to short crust pastry.

Ingredients

8 ozs plain flour
4 ozs unsalted butter

1 tablespoonful castor sugar
1 small measure of brandy
A little milk to mix

For the filling

8 ozs strawberries
4 ozs chocolate flakes
raspberry jam
4 egg whites
6 tablespoons castor sugar
3 or 4 drops of lemon juice

Method

Preheat oven to 425°F/220°C or Gas No. 7. Make pastry, leave to chill for one hour. Roll out and bake blind until just cooked, then lower heat to 325°F/170°C or Gas No. 3. Once cooked, take shell and spread raspberry jam over the base of the tart. Whisk egg whites until firm peaks, add lemon juice and sugar and fold in strawberries, left whole. Spoon strawberry mixture into the pastry case and bake for roughly 30 minutes, or until the meringue has taken a good colour. When cool, decorate with chocolate flakes.

I like to buy trays of apricots at this time of the year. Fresh apricot jam is wonderful, and so is apricot chutney. Here is a super delicious pie.

Apricot & Almond Pie

Ingredients

1¹/₂lbs fresh apricots (stoned)
3 tablespoons Kirsch or apricot brandy
1 tablespoon cornflour
3 ozs flaked almonds
A little castor sugar

For the rough puff pastry, or you can cheat and buy a packet.

8 ozs plain flour
3 ozs lard and
3 ozs margarine
Squeeze of lemon juice
Pinch of salt
Water to mix

Method

Cook apricots until just soft, drain, keeping the juice, and pile high on a large pie plate. Heat the juice in a pan with Kirsch and cornflour until thickened. Cool slightly. Pour over apricots and sprinkle with the flaked almonds.

To make rough puff pastry:

Mix flour and salt into mixing bowl, cut fat into $1/2$" cubes and add to the flour. Mix to a stiff dough with cold water, to which a squeeze of lemon has been added. Sprinkle flour on pastry board and roll the dough to an oblong length of about $1/2$" thickness, fold the pastry into three, lightly pressing the edges together. Give pastry half a turn, roll again, fold as before. Put in a cold place to rest for 20 minutes, then repeat twice more with pastry. Put pastry over the apricots. Decorate to please yourself, brush with a little beaten egg or milk. Sprinkle with caster sugar. Bake in oven 425°F/220°C or gas mark 7.

When I had my radio programme "Peggy's Patch", each week I used to give out recipes, and listeners would send in to me their favourite recipes. The following lines will make you smile. (I can't even tell you what oven temperature to use).

Recipe for Happiness

Ingredients

4 cups of love
2 cups of loyalty
3 cups of forgiveness
1 cup of friendship
2 spoonfuls of hope
2 spoonfuls of tenderness
4 quarts of faith
1 barrel of laughter

Method

Take love and loyalty
Mix thoroughly with faith
Blend in tenderness, kindness and understanding
Add friendship and hope
Sprinkle abundantly with laughter
Bake with sunshine
Serve daily with generous helpings.

With my radio programme you can well understand that I made many friends. Often people would ask me to go and look at their gardens. I used to, and still do, open garden fêtes, flower shows, bazaars and I also do presentations. So often my telephone rings and it's usually someone asking me a query, such as "Why won't their jam set", or "have I got a good recipe for Suffolk Rusks". One query which I get every year over the telephone and from people sending in their letters to me is, "when can I pickle walnuts"?, so I thought I would give you my recipe. A few years ago I was so disappointed, a lady brought me a large bag of green walnuts, "there", she said, "you can pickle these", but they were so hard I could not get a needle into them. So be warned, you must pick walnuts early in June. Use immature green nuts, if you leave it any later the vinegar will not penetrate the nut. Always wear rubber gloves when picking walnuts, as the stain is very difficult to remove.

Pickling Walnuts

You will need green walnuts, cooking salt and spiced vinegar. Prick the walnuts with a strong knitting needle, make a brine using

4 ozs salt and 2 pints of water to each 2lbs of walnuts. Soak the walnuts for 3 - 4 days. Then drain and cover with fresh brine and leave for one week. Drain thoroughly and spread out on a large dish (I use a large old meat dish) for about 24 hours. You will notice that the walnuts turn black. Put into pickle jars, pour over hot spiced vinegar and cover. When cold store in a cool place for 5 - 6 weeks before use. If you don't want to use spiced vinegar, try this sweet spiced one.

Ingredients

3 pints malt vinegar
1lb brown sugar
1¹/₂ level teaspoonful salt
1 level teaspoonful whole mixed spice
¹/₂ level teaspoonful whole cloves
1 level teaspoonful peppercorns

Method

Put the vinegar and spices into a pan and bring to the boil. Pour into a bowl and cover with a plate to preserve the flavour and leave for 2 hours. Then strain the vinegar and use as required. Remember, for all pickles, lids should be plastic lined, if not, the vinegar will eat into the lids if they are made of tin.

If you have a ploughman's supper with your pickled walnuts, you will need a drink to wash it down, so let's have a glass of Apple Ale.

Apple Ale

Ingredients

2lbs apples
1 gallon cold water
1$^{1}/_{2}$lbs sugar
1 oz bruised root ginger
$^{1}/_{2}$ teaspoonful cinnamon
$^{1}/_{2}$ teaspoonful cloves
1 orange

Method

Wash apples and grate them (I put mine into my food processor) complete with skins, add pulp to the water with juice and grated peel of the orange. Stir the apple water every day for 6 days, then strain, add sugar, root ginger, cinnamon and cloves. Stir until the sugar has dissolved and leave another 2 days. Then strain through muslin or a strong clean cloth. Pour into bottles, cork lightly and leave for a week, then it should be ready for drinking.

Another nice apple recipe which was sent to me from a lady who had been given it from her pen pal in Denmark, is **Danish Apple Pudding.**

Ingredients

1$^{1}/_{2}$lbs cooking apples peeled and sliced
4 ozs sugar

6 ozs brown bread
4 ozs butter
4 ozs demerara sugar
$1/2$ teaspoon ground nutmeg
$1/2$ teaspoon ground cinnamon
$1/4$ pint whipped cream
2 ozs grated chocolate

Method

Gently cook the apples with the sugar and very little water until soft. Mash to a puree and set aside to cool. Turn the bread into crumbs. Fry the crumbs in butter until crisp. Cool them and mix with the demerara sugar and spices in a bowl. Butter a 2 pint glass dish. Make a layer of crumbs on the base of the dish and cover with a layer of apples. Continue until the dish is filled, finishing with the crumbs. Chill for 12 hours. Spread whipped cream over the top of the pudding and sprinkle with grated chocolate. This pudding can be frozen and serves 6.

This is another favourite recipe from my Radio Programme -
Toffee Apples

Ingredients

12 small eating apples
1lb white or brown sugar
2 ozs butter
1 tablespoon golden syrup
2 teaspoons vinegar
$1/4$ pint water

Method

Wash and dry the apples. Push a stick into each apple (stalk end). Put all the remaining ingredients into a large pan and stir over a gentle heat until the sugar has dissolved, then boil rapidly for 5 minutes.

The syrup in the pan has to boil until it comes to the hard ball stage. This means that when a little of the syrup is dropped in some cold water it forms a hard ball; this allows you to know when it is toffee.

Continue to boil until this point is reached. Remove pan from the heat and as quickly as possible, dip the apples. Twirl them around in the toffee for a few seconds. Shake off the surplus and stand on a greased baking tin to set.

We all know that fruits make pleasant drinks for general use. When fruit was freshly gathered, the juice could easily be made into a refreshing cordial by adding sugar and hot water. For winter use it was customary to make fruit vinegars, which were used for delicious hot drinks. Years ago no country cottage pantry would have been without fruit vinegars. These vinegars were delicious hot, and thought to be a good antidote for winter colds. Any soft fruit could be used and the method was the same for each one. The following flavours were most highly prized.

Raspberry Vinegar

Ingredients

2lbs raspberries
2 pints red wine vinegar

Method

Put raspberries into a large bowl and pour the vinegar over them. Cover with a cloth and allow to stand for a week. Strain the raspberries and measure the juice. Put the juice into a pan and boil it for 5 minutes. Take juice off the heat and stir in 1lb sugar to each pint of liquid. Heat and stir until sugar is all dissolved. Do not allow to boil again, just let it cool before bottling. Cork firmly. To use, dilute with equal parts of boiling water to make a winter drink.

Blackberry vinegar can be made using the same method. This is a good way to use up ripe fruit.

For coughs and colds Elder Rob was made. One has to pick the fruits in summer and autumn to make these wonderful drinks. Elder Rob was, and still is, a good cough cure.

Elder Rob

Gather a good bowl full of elderberries. Bring berries to the boil, then simmer for 45 minutes. Strain through muslin and to each 1 pint of juice add 1lb demerara sugar. Also tie 4 cloves in muslin together with a good piece of root ginger. Put with sugar and juice, simmer for another 30 minutes, remove the spices after 15 minutes. Strain and bottle when cold.

For a soothing mixture for coughs, dilute 2 tablespoons Elder Rob with 1 tablespoon honey in a glass of hot water.

Whilst I am writing about fruit vinegars, we must not forget **herbal vinegars**. They bring a delicious new taste to salads and pickles. You can make any herb into a herbal vinegar, all you have to do, is chop a herb into small pieces and add as much vinegar as your jar or bottle will take. Leave the herb to infuse for 2 or 3 weeks, shaking the bottle every time you are in your kitchen or passing the bottles. Taste the vinegar for flavour, when the time is up strain the liquid from the herb through a cotton or muslin cloth, then take a fine sprig of the herb and place it in the flavoured vinegar.

A wine vinegar, I think, makes the best herbal vinegar. It's like all recipes, if you use the best ingredients, you get the best in flavour.

Basil flavoured vinegar is one I would not like to be without. In the winter I use it for salads as I find it gives that little extra lift.

Remember, all fruit and herbal vinegars should be kept in a dark cupboard to prevent loss of colour.

Another country savoury I love to make is mushroom ketchup. Sadly we don't see mushrooms growing in the pastures, as we did in years gone by. As children we would go and pick large field mushrooms, where the horses were grazing. It was well known that the best mushrooms picked, flourished where horses' manure had been dropped. Today you may see mushrooms growing in a meadow, but you should never pick them without getting the farmer's permission.

You need the large black ones for making ketchup, as they yield plenty of highly flavoured juice. Look in the markets, you may be able to get a basketful cheap as the market is closing for the day. Mushroom ketchup is so useful for flavouring soups, stews and casseroles.

Mushroom Ketchup

Ingredients

3lbs mushrooms
4 ozs salt
1 teaspoon fresh ground pepper
1 pint red wine vinegar
1 teaspoon pickling spice tied in muslin

Method

No need to wash the mushrooms, simply remove the base of the stalks and wipe the caps with a damp cloth. Break them into pieces and put them into a bowl and sprinkle with salt. Leave covered for 3 days, then strain off excess liquid from the mushrooms. Put mushrooms into a saucepan with pickling spice, pepper and vinegar and simmer for about ¹/₂ hour. Allow to cool, then strain into a jug. (I add 2 tablespoons of port to my ketchup, it gives it a little extra kick, I think!), then bottle. You may think the ketchup is rather thin, but this is to use as a flavour and not as a thick sauce.

HINTS & QUERIES

Hints on Using Cream

Single Cream
Traditionally used as a pouring cream, but is ideal for cooking especially in sauces, soups and hot dishes. Remember, however, that it will not whip.

Soured Cream
Don't be put off by the name - it is soured by adding a natural culture like the one used in yoghurt. This pungent cream is excellent for savoury dishes such as dips and sauces and can be used in scones, bread and cakes.

Whipping Cream
The most economical of all creams, as when whipped, it will double in volume and is particularly good for decorating and filling cakes, pastries and cold puddings. It pipes beautifully and is suitable for freezing.

Double Cream
The most popular and versatile of all fresh creams. It whips up to $1^{1/2}$-times its own volume and will hold its shape for up to 24 hours if chilled. Freezes well when whipped.

Tips for uses of cream - remember to add cream at the end of cooking. Stir in gently to prevent separation or curdling. Never add whipped cream to a warm mixture, as it will collapse and deflate. Whipping - for best results, pour cream into a chilled, clean bowl large enough to take four times the volume of the cream. This will allow air to be incorporated easily while whisking. Double cream will whip more readily and give a greater volume if 1-tablespoon of milk is added to every 140ml ($^1/4$ pint) cream. Sifted icing sugar, whipped with cream, gives better holding results - add 1 - 2 teaspoons to 140ml ($^1/4$ pint) cream. Whipping cream is the most commonly frozen.

Questions Posed & Answered

Q. Please, I so often forget to soak my bacon for boiling overnight to reduce the saltiness. What can I do ?

A. Put bacon in a pan, cover with cold water and bring to the boil. Pour away the cooking water and replace with fresh, cold water. Bring to the boil again, reduce the heat and simmer as usual.

Q. The question of blanching was brought up by some East Anglian Daily Times readers, asking if you need to blanch vegetables for the freezer.

A. Blanching destroys enzymes in the vegetables which causes deterioration of colour, flavour and texture. Blanching also forces air out of vegetables and this gives brighter colours.

Q. When people go on holiday they worry about leaving houseplants to become dry. What do they do ?

Taste of the Country Seasons

A. Put an old towel in the bottom of the bath, soaking the towel in water. Stand all the plants on the towel to absorb the moisture gradually.

Q. Why is it my preserves turn out unsuccessfully ?

A. One reason could be the use of over-ripe fruit. Another too short or too long boiling after addition of sugar which will give a syrupy consistency, also when sugar crystals form on top of jam, it could be because of under-boiling or too little acid.

Q. Why does jam often turn brownish in colour or cloudy ?

A. This could be due to using poor fruit, overcooking after the addition of sugar, storage too warm or too light.

Q. Jelly will sometimes go cloudy - why ?

A. Maybe you have been in too much of a hurry and to hasten the process, you have either squeezed the jelly bag or not used good quality fruit.

Q. Why does my fruit rise in the jar ?

A. Preserves not allowed to cool to about 76°C/170°F before potting or the jars are too hot when filling.

Q. What can I do with my jam if it has not set ?

A. Try tipping it back into the pan, re-boiling with extra lemon juice, but if that fails, use it as fruit sauce for ice-cream or hot puddings.

Country Hints

1. To keep cauliflower white when cooking, add a tablespoon of milk to the water.

2. Mushrooms plunged into boiling water for a minute or so, before frying or grilling, will be more succulent and will not shrivel.

3. A teaspoonful of lemon or orange juice added to cake mixture helps the cake to rise and makes it lighter in texture.

4. Half a teaspoonful of seed tapioca added to the water when cooking rhubarb, plums, etc., makes a thick juice.

5. Line the biscuit tin with blotting paper it will absorb the moisture and keep the biscuits crisp.

6. Put a teaspoonful of semolina in with the flour it makes crisp pastry.

7. To prevent mould, place a lump of sugar in the cheese dish.

8. When boiling rice or spaghetti, add a knob of margarine or a tablespoonful of oil, to the water.

9.   The many uses of salt - a pinch stops the white running out of an egg which cracks while boiling; a   pinch   will   add flavour when percolating coffee; a little salt added to mustard will keep it moist for a long time; when making meringues, add a pinch of salt to the eggwhites to make them go further.

10. Don't forget, if you run out of icing sugar, you can make some by putting granulated sugar into the liquidiser.

11. Clean orange or lemon peel from the grater with a pastry brush.

12. Before putting blanched almonds on top of a fruit cake, soak them in milk for a minute then wipe them dry they will not burn or go brown while cooking.

The Suffolk Sausage

Over the years you see more and more people eating their meals outside during the summer months. A lot of houses are built with patios, and some even have built-in areas for cooking. I often wonder what my parents would have thought, as barbecues were never heard of, the only food they ate in the open air in their days, was food taken into the harvest fields, which consisted mostly of bread, cheese and cake.

Sausages are big business nowadays. Suffolk is very famous for the "banger", as it is known. Many butchers guard their secret recipes with their lives. Newmarket is famous for sausages. We have the *Good Food Guide* butchers in Woodbridge, who make wonderful sausages, also nearby my village is Wickham Market, where we have Mr. E.W. Revetts, whose sausages are delicious, and I know for a fact, people will travel 100 miles to buy his sausages. I buy 5lbs of them at a time, and both my sons will travel out from their respective villages to buy Mr. Revetts' sausages, they won't eat any other brand. There is something about his spices and herbs which give his sausages a special flavour. However, if you have the time, I will give a homemade recipe, and you don't have to have sausage skins, just roll the mixture into sausage shapes. This recipe will make about a pound of sausages.

Peggy's Sausages

Ingredients

1lb of belly of pork meat
2 small eggs beaten

6 - 8 ozs soft breadcrumbs
1 tablespoon small fresh sage leaves chopped
Salt and pepper to taste
A little flour for rolling
Some dripping for frying

Method

Remove rind from pork, cut meat into small chunks, then mince mixture thoroughly with egg, sage and seasonings with enough breadcrumbs to form a soft rollable mixture. With floured hands roll suitable quantities of the mixture into sausage shapes. Fry gently in a little dripping, turning frequently until brown all over.

These sausages will not cost you less than the shop bought ones, but once you have tasted them, you will want to repeat them again and again. The taste will make the work involved all worthwhile, but do buy good quality pork as you want a good flavour.

Most men love a good meat pie or meat pudding, and I have noticed that a lot of our local pubs have increased puddings on their menu boards. So, puddings have made a come back very much during the last few years, and I do mean the old fashioned steam puddings.

My mother used to make wonderful bacon and onion suet puddings. As you can imagine there was not much meat, but bacon pieces were cheap and they made a good pudding and filled us children up. Another pie she made was, Meat and Potato Pie. You will guess by the recipe that there was more vegetables than meat. But first I would like to give you this little story about the Rat & Sparrow Club, given to me by a radio fan. When I told it to old ladies in the village, they soon told me how they used to make sparrow pies in years gone by.

History of the Rat & Sparrow Club

Years ago the farmers of Kent, realising the damage the rats and sparrows were doing on the farms, offered a prize to the farmhand who collected the most rats tails and sparrows heads in the year - thus the Rat & Sparrow Club was formed. Every Sunday morning the members of this club would meet to catch rats and sparrows. They saved the rats tails and sparrows heads, and once every week would meet at the local pub where a tally was recorded for each member. Once a year they all met at a pre-arranged hostelry for the presentation of cups to the member with the most rat tails and sparrow heads caught during the year, after they had consumed a good meal of Steak and Kidney Pudding and plenty of ale. A further prize was awarded to the best tale told, no females were present! Whether this club still exists today, I do not know.

Meat & Potato Pie

As I have said, the cheapest meat was always used, but for this pie you need $^3/4$lb stewing beef, salt and pepper, $1^1/2$lbs mixed vegetables, all diced. Onions, potatoes and carrots and any other vegetables that you have. Plus a few herbs.

Method
Cook meat first on a slow hob until tender, then put the meat, diced vegetables and herbs into a pie dish, fill $^3/4$ full with a stock made from beef cubes. Make a crust with the following:-

³/₄lb plain flour
1 teaspoon baking powder
6 ozs dripping or fat

Make up the crust by rubbing dripping into flour and baking powder, mix with a little water. Roll out pastry to fit pie dish. First cut a strip to go round the edge of the pie dish (wet the edges first). Put a pie funnel in the middle of the dish of meat and vegetables, then lay a lid of pastry on top, sealing it round the edges. Make a hole in the centre of pastry lid, to let the steam out, and brush over with a little milk or beaten egg. Bake in a moderate oven for ³/₄ to 1 hour.

Here are three more sweets from my friends, which are very popular. This one is called "Perry's" Chocolate Souffle. Sometimes she changes the chocolate for coffee by dissolving 2 tablespoons of coffee in a little water.

Perry's Chocolate Soufflé

Ingredients

4 eggs
1 large tin evaporated milk
3 ozs castor sugar
2 tablespoons cocoa
2 sachets gelatine

Method

Leave the milk in fridge for at least 2 hours before using. Whip egg whites until stiff, whip milk until thick, whip egg yolks with sugar until thick, dissolve gelatine in hot water, mix cocoa in hot water and add cocoa to egg mixture and whisk well. Add gelatine and whisk well again. In a large bowl place the egg whites, milk and chocolate mixture. Using a large metal spoon, fold together until well mixed. When cold, grate plain chocolate on top of souffle and decorate with fresh cream.

Perry is a good cook. Like myself she is self taught. She takes on catering, sometimes providing meals for up to 150 - 200 people. She caters for weddings, and makes wedding cakes and goes to evening classes, to learn the Sugar Guild Icing technique. Some of her decorated cakes look too good to cut and eat. I remember when Thora Hurd came to do a T. V. programme "Praise Be" from my garden, Perry made a cake for her and decorated it with iced primroses. Thora was so thrilled with it. Perry gets orders from the surrounding villages for all sorts of cakes, including lots of birthday and anniversary cakes. Jill always brings her Chocolate Roulade when we have a party or some fund raising event for our Church, and believe me, it's a headache to know what to do sometimes to raise money. When I have coach parties to visit my garden and they ask me to book teas for them, Jill will get the ladies from our Church together. She will hire the village hall well in advance, and do cream teas and scones, and this all helps towards our Church funds.

Our Women's Institute does Ploughman's Suppers, and this also helps to raise funds. This way of raising funds has caught on in a lot of villages around my area. Most visitors enjoy a homemade tea or ploughman's supper and it helps to bring money into our villages.

When we have our over 60s Christmas Party each year, we do a wide range of sweets, and Jill's Chocolate Roulade is always one of the first sweets to go.

Jill's Chocolate Roulade

Ingredients:-

6 ozs block chocolate
5 eggs
8 ozs castor sugar
3-4 tablespoons water

For filling:-

$^1/2$ pint double cream (lightly whipped and flavoured with vanilla essence, or rum or brandy)
Icing sugar for dusting
One shallow Swiss roll tin 12 inches long x 8 inches wide, or a roulade case

Line tin with oiled greaseproof paper, or brush the paper case with oil or melted shortening. Set oven temperature at 350°F/180°C or Gas Mark 4.

Method

Separate the eggs, beat the yolks with the sugar adding them gradually until the mixture is lemon coloured. Melt chocolate in water in a pan over a gentle heat and, when it is a thick cream, draw pan aside. Whip the eggs to a firm snow, then add chocolate to egg yolk mixture. Cut and fold egg whites into the mixture and turn it into the prepared tin. Place in pre-set moderate oven and bake for 10-15 minutes or until firm to the touch.

Have ready a clean cloth, which has been wrung out in cold water. Take out the roulade, cool it slightly and cover with the cloth. (This is to prevent any sugary crust forming). Leave it in a cool place for 12 hours or in a refrigerator overnight.

Lay a piece of greaseproof paper on table, dust it well with icing sugar. Remove the cloth and turn roulade upside down onto prepared paper. Remove tin. Spread it with whipped cream and roll up like a Swiss roll. Lift onto serving dish and dust well with icing sugar.

❦

Win lives nearby me, and used to do so much for the Horticultural Society at Battisford, also helping to raise money for other events. When I had lunch recently with both her and her husband, she gave me the following recipe.

Banana Chartreuse
(I call it Win's Banana Sweet)

Ingredients

1 pkt Rowntrees lime jelly
5 bananas
Juice of $1/2$ lemon
$3/4$ pint of double cream

Method

Measure $^1/4$ pint water into a saucepan and bring to the boil. Break jelly and add to hot water, stirring until dissolved, add $^1/2$ pint of cold water and stir, spoon a little into the container you are going to make the Chartreuse in, put in fridge to chill and set, then put the remainder of the jelly into fridge.

Slice up one of the bananas and arrange around the edge of jelly in the container, then gently spoon a little more jelly over, taking care not to disturb the banana.

Place the remainder of the bananas into a bowl and mash them with the lemon juice. Place the cream in another bowl and beat until thick. Then beat in the remainder of the jelly, which should by now be almost set, then fold into the mashed banana. Spoon this into the container on top of the sliced banana and jelly, chill until firm.

Just before serving, dip in a bowl of hot water for a minute to loosen, then place a round tray or dish over the container, turn over and lift container away.

This can be served with a bowl of fresh cream, if so wished. Can be made over night and left in container.

Going around giving my talks you can imagine that I meet lots people and have made many friends, and they call in to see me when they are in my area. One lady I met from Aldeburgh, named Gwen, works in the Aldeburgh Hospital looking after elderly day patients. When I went and showed them the slides of my garden they thoroughly enjoyed looking at them. I often visit Old People's Homes and show them slides of the countryside, my garden or the making of the Akenfield film. Gwen is a Scottish lass - she makes lots of homemade goodies to sell to raise money for her Day Centre, and this is one of the recipes she gave to me.

"Sweet Treat" Scottish Tablet

(very moreish)

Ingredients

1lb granulated sugar
$1/2$ pint water or milk
2 ozs butter
1 small can condensed milk
1 teaspoon vanilla essence

Method

Lightly grease a 7 inch square cake tin. Dissolve sugar and water or milk in a thick based pan making a syrup. Add butter and condensed milk, heat gently and bring to boil, stirring continuously for 40 - 50 minutes. Test tablet by dropping a little syrup in a cup of cold water, if it forms a soft ball it's ready. Take off heat, add essence, beat mixture until mixture grains and thickens (it is important to beat it well). Pour into tin and cut into squares when cold and set. Makes $1^{1/2}$lb of tablet.

Mincemeat Cake

Ingredients

7 ozs S.R. wholemeal flour
4 ozs butter

4 ozs Barbados sugar
3 large eggs
12 ozs mincemeat
4 tablespoons milk

Method

Line 8 inch round cake tin with greaseproof paper. Cream butter and sugar well, beat in eggs, one at a time with a little of the flour. Stir in mincemeat and fold in flour, add milk to get a moist mixture. Bake at 325°F/170°C or Gas Mark 3 for 10 minutes, then lower heat to 300°F/150°C or Gas Mark 2 for about $1^{1}/4$ hours until cake is firm on top and shrinking away from the sides of tin slightly. Leave to cool before removing from tin.

I think this would make a nice cake for Christmas.

Singing Johnny (Liqueur)

Ingredients

Half a bottle of whisky
1 cup of raspberries
1 cup of granulated sugar

Method

Put all the ingredients in a non-metallic container and leave for 6 months. Strain out raspberries, which will now be white. Bottle liqueur - the raspberries can be used in a trifle.

In years gone by, no matter how short of money the housewife was, she would never neglect to fill the store cupboard. The winters were long and cold. I remember my mother used to bottle jar after jar of fruit. Apple rings were dried, pickles and chutneys made, and even chicken's eggs were preserved in water glass (she never pickled eggs in vinegar). A pail stood on the pantry floor - it looked like white limewash jelly. Eggs would have been put into this liquid in the summer time when chickens were laying well. Mother used the eggs for baking and cooking. There would have always been a corner in the house or spare bedroom, for storing a supply of potatoes, onions and apples. Remember, cottage gardens were large, so that plenty of shallots, beetroots and red cabbages were grown for pickling, not forgetting green tomatoes. The work of pickling only entailed "picking and boiling up". The ingredients were cheap, and all that was really needed, was the time to do the pickling. I feel today that young people don't want the bother of these homely tasks, there are other more interesting things to do, like watching television, playing squash, so why bother, when you can buy a jar of pickled onions without the tedious peeling process. But you get the commercial pickled onion and the home pickled onion together on a plate and I bet you can tell the difference in flavour.

I will now give you a few preserve recipes from the countryside.

Crab Apple Jelly

Ingredients

4lbs Crab apples

My home-made preserves

2 - 3lbs granulated sugar
3 pints water
1 lemon

Method

Wash and cut apples in halves and cook in water until soft. Strain off the juice through a piece of butter muslin. Tie the remaining pulp in the muslin and suspend it over the bowl of juice to drip overnight. (Could I just say at this point, with all jellies, do not squeeze the muslin or the jelly will become cloudy). Throw away the pulp. Put the juice in a preserving pan with 1lb of sugar to each pint of juice and juice of a lemon. Boil until it jells (about 20 minutes).

Another preserve I enjoy making is **Sloe and Apple Jelly**. Once more, the fruit is free, if you know where to look for it. The sloe is very bitter, but it blends well with apples.

Ingredients

4lbs apples (windfalls will do)
2lbs sloes
1lb sugar to each pint of juice
Cold water

Method

Wash all fruit, removing any stalks. Cut the apples into pieces. Do not peel them or remove cores. Put fruit into pan and cover with water, boil until soft. Strain fruit through muslin and put the juice into a pan with 1lb of sugar to each pint of juice. Boil until it jells - about 15 minutes. Pot up and seal immediately.

We must not forget the blackberry. You can make so much with this berry, it may be seedy, but the wild blackberry is much superior to the cultivated variety. Blackberry and apple is one of my favourite jams.

Blackberry & Apple Jam

You need equal weights of apples and blackberries and 1lb of sugar to each pound of fruit and $1/2$ pint of water. Peel apples and cut up small. Check blackberries and put all the fruit into pan with water. Simmer slowly until apples are cooked and all the fruit is tender. Dissolve sugar in this pulp. Boil briskly for about $1/4$ of an hour. Put into jars and seal.

As autumn creeps in we may walk the country lanes and see the changing colours, and if we walk across the meadows in damp weather we may find some field mushrooms. I have written about mushroom picking and making mushroom ketchup earlier in this book, however, here is another way of preserving mushrooms.

Pickled Mushrooms

Ingredients

1lb mushrooms
Salt water to cover

1 pint malt vinegar
1 medium sized onion
2 garlic cloves bruised (if liked)

Method

Tie 9-10 bruised pepper corns, 3 bay leaves, 2 sprigs of rosemary and the 2 garlic cloves in a piece of muslin. Bring the mushrooms to the boil in the salted water and remove from the heat. Allow to stand for 5 minutes before draining off. Dry the mushrooms on kitchen paper. Simmer the vinegar with the herbs and spices for 15 minutes, then cool and strain. Pack the mushrooms into a wide necked jar, pour spiced vinegar over the mushrooms. Seal and store for 2-3 weeks before eating. (Super with a crusty roll and cheese).

I wonder if, while I am still talking about mushrooms, you have thought of eating puff ball. The giant puff ball will be found growing on pastures, sometimes on golf courses, grassy roadsides and woodlands (they are often found in the same spot in successive years). The flesh is firm and white, later turning yellowish and finally brown and powdery. You need to eat it when young, whilst the flesh is white and firm. It is excellent when thickly sliced and fried in bacon fat until golden brown. You can also cut it up and use it in other dishes, such as stews, casseroles and soups. It is said that years ago the yellowish powder from a puff ball was used to stop bleeding at amputations.

Another free gift from the countryside that can be found at this time of the year, is the hazelnut. The best time to gather these nuts is when they are turning brown, usually towards the end of

September. They are ripe if they fall from the husks when the tree is shaken.

I feel very fortunate, for in my son Allan's garden, cultivated hazelnuts (Kentish Cob) grow in the border. Each year he brings me a large bag full, which I use in my Christmas puddings, cakes and sweets - they soon break up if you put them in a food processor for a few minutes, and here is a favourite recipe of mine.

Hazelnut Meringue

Ingredients

4ozs finely chopped hazelnuts
3ozs castor sugar
3 ozs icing sugar
3 egg whites
A pinch of salt

Method

Take a bowl and put in nuts, castor and icing sugar together with a pinch of salt. In another bowl whisk egg whites until stiff, then fold in dry ingredients. Place in a wellbuttered oven-proof dish. Put dish on middle shelf in oven and bake at 225°F/110°C or Gas Mark $1/4$ for $2^{1}/2$ hours, until the meringue is crisp.

Another tasty pie, using vegetables and nuts, can be served if you don't have any meat, and I sometimes think it's good to have a dish of mixed vegetables. Some people would say "where is the meat?", but once they had tasted this pie, they would be back for a second helping, and here it is.

Hazelnut Pie with vegetables

Ingredients

1 lb potatoes
6 ozs chopped hazelnuts
2 medium sized onions
4 ozs mushrooms
2 tablespoons chopped parsley
1 teaspoon chopped fresh thyme
2-3 ozs butter or margarine
A little milk and a few breadcrumbs

Method

Cook the potatoes and mash with milk. Season with salt and pepper and a little butter. Slice and fry onions in a little butter until just golden, add sliced mushrooms and fry a further minute or two. Mix into the mashed potatoes together with the nuts, thyme and parsley. Bind with a little milk and place in a well-greased pie dish. Sprinkle the top with breadcrumbs and dot with butter.

Bake at 350°F/180°C or gas mark No. 4 for about $1/2$ hour.

Years ago the damson was another fruit which used to be found in most cottage gardens, and if you are lucky, you can still find it growing wild in some parts of the country. One of the best varieties is called Merryweather. It is an excellent all-round performer and has a blue-black skin, yellow flesh, which is juicy, and a good spicy tart flavour. It is used for cooking jams and wine making. Try this recipe.

Damson & Walnut Jam

Ingredients

4lbs damsons
4 pints water
4lbs sugar
10 ozs walnut pieces

Method

Put damsons and water into a preserving pan and simmer gently until soft. Remove stones as they appear (this is a fiddly and messy job). Add sugar and boil rapidly for about 10 minutes. Add the walnut pieces and boil for a further 2 minutes, or until setting point is reached. Pot into warm jars and seal.

You can make Damson Cheese, which means leaving out the walnuts and simmering the damsons and sugar longer, when you should end up with a thick cheese, which is very good served with cold meats or Stilton cheese.

Quince is another fruit worth cultivating if you have the room for a tree. Stewed quinces are delicious and much finer than stewed pears. I often get telephone calls from readers of my weekly column in the East Anglian Daily Times, asking if Quince Jelly can be made out of the fruits of Japonica (or Cydonia). This is the flowering shrub which has large seed fruits; they are very hard and turn yellow when ripe. Yes, you can make a nice jelly with these fruits, but the real quince has an aromatic flesh, and when making an apple pie, a few slices of quince added to it will give it a superb flavour.

Sadly, you don't see this fruit in the shops, but we have a lady who brings this fruit to sell at our Women's Institute Market each year in October. There is always a rush to buy this fruit. The quinces are shaped like a large pear, and too hard and bitter to be eaten fresh. You should store quinces well away from other foods.

Quince Jelly

Ingredients

2lbs quinces
3 pints water
1lb sugar to each pint of juice
2 lemons

Method:

Cut up the fruit and simmer with water and lemon juice. This may take about 1 hour. Strain liquid through a muslin cloth and allow 1lb sugar to 1 pint juice. Boil until setting point is reached. Pot up in warm jars and seal.

Here are some recipes for that underrated vegetable the pumpkin.

Pumpkin & Cream Cheese Pâté

Ingredients

Cook some pumpkin in a little water and then drain well and puree. For 8 ozs purée allow 4 ozs cream cheese, 2 teaspoon anchovy essence, 1 crushed clove of garlic, salt, mustard and pepper to taste. 1 oz butter

Method:

Liquidize or beat well together and put into suitable dish. Serve with brown bread and green salad.

Pumpkin Pickle

Ingredients

1 small pumpkin
1 quart white vinegar
$1/2$ oz ground ginger
$1/2$ oz caster sugar

Method

Peel the pumpkin and remove the seeds and pith and cut into small dice. Steep for 12 hours in brine. Boil the vinegar, sugar and ginger for 10 minutes. Drain the pumpkin and add it to the vinegar. Boil for a further 10 minutes and then pour into sterilized jars and cover and label.

Pumpkin Cheesecake

Ingredients

8 oz flan pastry
jam
8 ozs pumpkin purée
8 ozs cream cheese
4 ozs sugar
2 eggs
rind of 1 lemon
vanilla essence

Method

Line a 10 inch flan tin with the pastry and spread with a thin layer of jam. Whip together all other ingredients and pile into pastry case. Cook at 375°F/190°C or Gas Mark 5 until set and golden. Leave until cold and then decorate with whipped cream.

Three Fruit Chutney

Ingredients

¹/₂lb pumpkin
¹/₂lb cooking pears
¹/₂lb cooking apples
1 oz chopped onion

$1/2$ teaspoon flour
$1/2$ teaspoon dry mustard
$1/4$ oz cayenne pepper
$1/4$ oz turmeric
$1/4$ oz ground ginger
$1/2$ pint vinegar
4 to 6 ozs white sugar

Method

Prepare pumpkin, sprinkle with salt and leave overnight. Pour off liquid, steam and mash with a fork. Cook apples, pears and onion in as little water as possible until soft, then mash with a fork. Put one-third of vinegar and all the other ingredients, except sugar, into a pan and simmer until thick. Add rest of vinegar and warmed sugar and simmer until thick. Chutney is ready if no liquid is visible when a wooden spoon is drawn through the mixture. Pot and cover.

Another Jill in our village, who, whenever the Church has a party or a harvest supper, is the one to organise cooking the food. Pumpkin bread is one of her specialities.

Pumpkin Bread

Ingredients

3 cups white flour
$3^{1/2}$ cups plain flour
$1/2$ teaspoon baking powder
2 teaspoons bicarbonate of soda

$1^{1}/_{2}$ *teaspoons salt*
1 teaspoon each cinnamon, nutmeg and cloves
1 cup of oil
1 cup of water
2 cups of pumpkin pulp
4 eggs

Method

Mix all dry ingredients together in a bowl. Then mix remaining ingredients well. Add the dry ingredients to the oil mixture and mix well. Pour into 2 prepared 2lb loaf tins. Bake at 325°F/170°C, Gas Mark 3 for about 1 hour. When partially cooled, wrap well in foil to keep moist.

Here is another good way of using up your courgettes. This recipe was given to me by the late Joan Laurie, who was our Rector's wife, she was very adapt at making up good recipes. The Reverend Jim, as we call him, is a keen gardener and grows a lot of vegetables; he even keeps a few chickens, and they often had a surplus of eggs at various times of the year - hence courgette omelette.

Courgette Omelette
(devised by one who has only too many courgettes
and more than enough eggs!)

For each person you will need 2 eggs, about an ounce of cheese and 5 or 6 ozs of courgettes (when prepared for cooking).
Cook the courgettes in a little butter or oil or just in its own juice in a covered pan (but do let the liquid boil off at the end).

118

Tip into a bowl, add the beaten eggs, grated cheese, salt and pepper (preferably black and freshly ground). Stir well and tip into a frying pan, in which you have heated a little butter or oil. When it sets around the edges, loosen them and cover the pan, a plate upside down will do if you have no lid.

When the top is nearly set, in five or ten minutes, depending on size, put the pan under a hot grill to brown the top. (If your pan or its handle won't stand up to the heat, just let it cook covered until set).

Now you can either dish it up hot, by itself or with vegetables, or let it get cold, when it is excellent with salad or, of course, make a really big one and have it both ways.

Ginger

Ginger is one of the best stimulants which we have in domestic medicine. It is safe to use, pleasant to eat, and warming and comforting to the digestion. After a chill, or in order to prevent a cold, there is nothing better than a glass of ginger wine, or even to chew a lump of crystallised ginger. In cooking, ginger is almost as indispensable as cloves and nutmegs, and I am sure many people will agree that English gingerbread is delicious as a fruit cake.

The part of the plant which is used is the root, and the best roots comes from the West Indies. It is often called green ginger, which is the name given before the root is dried. In cooking, and also when making ginger tea, the root is used in powder form. The fresh root is sometimes grated and used on curry and we know what a difference added ginger makes to a slice of melon.

I have a jar of preserved ginger in my store cupboard, and when I make marmalade I add chopped ginger - this makes a delicious preserve. If you feel that you would like to make your own **preserved ginger**, try this recipe - but be warned it takes time.

Take 1lb fresh ginger roots, $1^{1/2}$ cups water, 1lb sugar. Scrub roots of fresh ginger using a brush. Pare with a sharp knife and place the roots at once in cold water. Rinse well and place in fresh cold water. Let stand overnight. Drain and weigh the ginger, then place it in a preserving kettle and cover it with cold water. Heat, and when the water is boiling, skim out the ginger and place it again in cold water. When it is quite cold, return to the kettle and add more cold water. When the water is boiling, skim out the ginger and place in cold water as before. Repeat this three times or until the ginger is tender. Boil the sugar and water together for 10 minutes. Drain the ginger, add it to the syrup, bring quickly to boiling point, remove from the heat and let it stand overnight. Drain off the syrup and let it come to the boil, then repeat the first process. Drain off the syrup again and bring to the boil, add the ginger and simmer until clear. Pour into hot jars and seal. In two weeks' time it will be ready for use.

Horseradish

I expect most people who have horseradish growing in the garden will be trying their best to get rid of it. It is a rather large plant belonging to the Cruciferae family, and, looking at it from a distance, you would think it was a large clump of dock leaves. The plant was thought to have come from Russia and has been given alternative names such as Breton Gunpowder and German Mustard, and believe me, it is much hotter than the jar you buy from the supermarket! The sauce made from the horseradish is very strong. When I first used it I put some in the processor, but when I lifted the lid I had to stand back, as the aroma was so strong my eyes soon filled with tears. However, it is very good to eat with beef, fish and poultry. Medicinally it was taken grated to assist digestion, and if you grate some over salads it should help to cure coughs and colds. If you feel a cold coming on, just stand over a bowl of grated horseradish and inhale the fumes which arise. When making bread sauce, a little grated or dried horseradish will give that little extra bite and taste to the sauce. When I can get a hold of some, I grate it and store it in a jar with some white vinegar, then when I need to make a sauce, I just take some out of the jar - it will store for a long time, using this method.

At first glance this recipe for **Bible Cake** looks like a riddle!

1. $1/2$lb Judges V.25 (Last Clause)

2. $1/2$lb Jeremiah vi,20

3. $1/2$ tablespoon Samuel xiv, 25

4. 3 tablespoons Jeremiah xvii, 11

5. $1/2$lb Nahum iii, 12

6. $1/2$ lb Samuel xxx, 12

7. 2 ozs Numbers xvii, 8 (blanched and chopped)

8. 1 lb Kings iv, 22

9. Season to taste with 11 Chronicles ix, 9

10. A pinch of Leviticus ii, 13

11. 1 tablespoon Amos iv, 5 (For Leaven read Baking Powder)

12. 3 tablespoons Judges iv, 19

Beat 1, 2 & 3 to a cream, add 4, one at a time, still beating, add 5, 6 & 7, beat again. Add 8, 9, 10 & 11, having previously mixed them and lastly, 12. Bake in a slow oven for $1^{1/2}$ hours.

I thought so too, but I looked in my Bible and found the ingredients to be as given below:-

1. $^{1/2}$lb butter

2. $^{1/2}$lb sugar

3. $^{1/2}$ tablespoon honey

4. 3 tablespoons beaten egg

5. $^{1/2}$lb figs

6. $^{1/2}$lb raisins

7. 2 ozs almonds

8. 1 lb flour

9. *Spice to taste*

10. *Pinch of salt*

11. *1 tablespoon baking powder (leaven)*

12. *3 tablespoons milk*

Try it!

❧

As autumn approaches, days are drawing in. Loads of logs are brought in (for those who still have open fires), and frost is in the air. Autumn has always been the time when we look at our stores in the outhouses and barns. We also need something to warm us up, so let's have......

Rich Potato Bake

Ingredients

1lb boiled potatoes
4 ozs bacon
1 onion
2 tablespoons milk
2 ozs grated cheese
1 oz dried bread crumbs
1 tin condensed mushroom soup
Salt and pepper to taste

Autumn

Method

Cut potatoes into thin slices, chop the bacon and fry it without fat until crisp. Finely chop the onion and cook until soft in the bacon fat. Mix the milk with the soup and season with salt and pepper. Arrange half the potatoes in a greased oven proof dish. Cover with bacon and onions and remainder of potatoes, pour the soup over the top and cover with mixed cheese and bread crumbs. Bake in a hot oven 450°F/230°C or Gas Mark 8 for 15 - 20 mins, until the top is golden brown.

This makes a nice supper dish after a hard day's work outside!

The swede vegetable is never very interesting cooked in the ordinary way, so try this way with bacon.

Swedes with Bacon

Take thin slices of smoked bacon and put a layer in the bottom of a saucepan, then a layer of swede, and so on in alternate layers until you have as much as is required. Then add 2 tablespoons of cold water and place at side of cooking stove and simmer gently until cooked. The swedes will stew in their own liquid and absorb the flavour of the bacon, and in consequence are much more delicious than when cooked in the usual way.

It's chutney and pickle time and here are a few tips for making the perfect pickle. Use a good sized stainless steel or well scoured aluminium pan. Not brass, copper or iron, the vinegar will corrode the metal. For the same reason use a wooden spoon and nylon sieve. Use the best vinegar. You can't make a good pickle without using good vinegar. Cider and wine vinegars will blend well with the more delicately spiced pickles. Spiced vinegar with a malt base is reliable, balanced and easy to use. Introduce extra flavour by steeping grated horseradish, slivers of orange or lemon rind, or a peeled garlic clove in a bottle of vinegar for a week or two before needed. Strain before using in recipe. Use white or brown sugar. White is better for pickles which needs no extra colour. Brown demerara or soft brown sugar gives a rich colour and deep flavour. Long slow cooking of the sugar will darken the chutney. Vine fruits like raisins will add extra sweetness to the finished product, so you may want to reduce the amount of sugar used in the recipe. Jam pot covers are no good, as vinegar will evaporate. Properly lined screw-top lids are best.

Bread & Butter Pickle

Ingredients

1 large cucumber
1/2lb onions skinned
5 level teaspoons salt
5 ozs granulated sugar
3/4 - 1 pint white distilled vinegar
1/2 level teaspoon each celery and mustard seeds

Method

Wash and thinly slice the cucumber. Thinly slice the onions and place in a large bowl and sprinkle over the salt. Leave for one hour. Rinse well and drain. Slowly dissolve the sugar in the vinegar. When completely dissolved add the celery and mustard seeds. Bring to the boil and bubble for 5 mins. Pack vegetables

Fresh from Akenfield Garden for chutney making

into warm jars, pour over the hot vinegar to completely cover. Seal in the usual way.

Tomato is another wonderful basic chutney ingredient providing bulk and colour, and a distinctive taste. If you want a hot spicy chutney, try tomato and red pepper.

Tomato & Red Pepper Chutney

Ingredients

4lbs ripe tomatoes
2 red chillies
1b onions
2 sweet red peppers
1 pint distilled vinegar
8 ozs demerara sugar
1 level teaspoon salt
2 level teaspoons paprika pepper
$^{1}/_{2}$ level teaspoon chilli powder

Method

Skin and roughly chop tomatoes, finely chop the chillies, skin and roughly chop the onions, halve, de-seed and chop the peppers. Place all the ingredients in a medium-sized pan and heat gently until the sugar dissolves. Boil gently, uncovered, until the vegetables are tender and the chutney is of a thick pulpy consistency, about $1^{1}/_{2}$ hours, stirring occasionally. Pot and cover in the usual way.

Eva was born in Poland and comes to the W.I. Market each week. She gave me this recipe for pear chutney which she makes every year.

Pear Chutney

Ingredients

4lbs pears finely chopped
1lb onions finely chopped
1lb tomatoes peeled and cut up
2 green peppers de-seeded
8 ozs raisins
1lb demerara sugar
2 cloves garlic crushed
$1/4$ teaspoon cayenne pepper
1 level teaspoon ground ginger
6 whole cloves
1 level teaspoon pickling spice
$1/2$ oz salt
$1^1/2$ pints pickling vinegar

Method

Cook prepared vegetables gently for 20 mins without any liquid, then add all the remaining ingredients (spices tied in muslin). Heat gently until thick, approximately $1^1/2$ hours. Remove spice bag and pot up. Makes about 5lbs.

Mixed Fruit Chutney

Ingredients

1lb green tomatoes or 1lb cooking apples
2 peeled bananas
8 ozs onions (chopped finely)
8 ozs raisins
4 ozs crystallised ginger (chopped finely)
2 teaspoons salt
1 teaspoon cayenne pepper
12 ozs brown sugar
1 pint white vinegar

Method

Cook altogether in a closed pan until tender, add $^1/2$ pint of water (if using apples) or $^1/4$ pint if using tomatoes. Add salt, cayenne pepper, sugar and vinegar. Simmer uncovered until the consistency is thick. Pot in warm jars and cover. A beautiful chutney.

Medlars

The medlar is one of England's oldest fruits and gone are the days when this fruit was eaten with port wine at dinner parties. The fruit is shaped like a large rounded rose hip and is the colour of unripe russet apples. They are normally left on the trees until late autumn and well after harvest. The fruit should be gathered and kept until they are soft and ripe, then the middle can be scooped out, mixed with a little sugar and cream and served as a dessert. Jam can also be made from medlars as follows:-

Medlar Jam

Ingredients

4 lbs medlars
Sugar
Vanilla pod

Method

Scrape the pulp from the fruit and cook gently, adding very little water so as not to burn. Sieve and weigh the pulp and add 12 ozs sugar for each 1lb fruit pulp. Put in the vanilla pod and boil together until setting point is reached. Take out the pod and pot up into warm jars. Medlar Jelly can also be made. For making a good homemade wine, you need ripe fruit with no green colour in the flesh. You will need 6lb fruit, 1lb raisins, juice and rind of one orange, nutrients: pectic enzymes, yeast and $2^{1/2}$lbs sugar.

East Anglia is well known for its samphire or samfer, some even call it "Poor man's Asparagus". Many still regard it as a speciality. Local people still squelch through the mud to gather bright green fleshy spikes. This salty wild vegetable's season is from July to September. It grows in the salt marshes near the coast. The method of serving has not changed down the years.
Once picked, place in a bucket of cold water and allow to stand for a few hours to get rid of most of the mud. Rinse in several pints of cold water, then place in a large pan, cover with cold

water and boil until tender (about 15 to 20 minutes). Drain and serve on a hot plate, it is then eaten by each person using their fingers to take a spike and dip it in melted butter or a vinegar dressing, the fleshy part is then sucked off each shoot. If you wish to pickle samphire, clean the samphire as above and dry it with a cloth. Put it in a bowl, boil some vinegar and pour enough of the vinegar to cover it and leave overnight. Drain, re-boil the vinegar, adding more if necessary, and pour over samphire while at boiling point. After five minutes, drain and pack samphire into jars with a sprig of tarragon. Cover with boiled vinegar and seal.

Another pickle which I make, is a Beer Pickle, this is used for pickling ham, pork or ox's tongues. It really does make a difference to your meat.

Beer Pickle

Ingredients

3 pints beer (old ale is best)
3 pints water
10 ozs salt
1 tablespoon saltpetre (this gives the meat a nice pink colour)
8 ozs black treacle
8 ozs brown sugar
1 oz crushed allspice

Method

Place all ingredients in a large pan with spice and tied in a piece of muslin. Bring to the boil and maintain boiling point for 5 minutes, as the scum comes to the top, skim off. Allow to cool. Place pieces of pork or tongue in the liquid and cover. Leave in pickle 7 to 10 days.

If you wish for a quick brine which will greatly improve a joint for 2 - 3 days try this recipe.

A Quick Brine

Ingredients

5 pints soft water
$3/4$ lb sea salt (other salt will do just as well)
$3/4$ lb brown sugar
2 ozs saltpetre

Method

Put all into a pan and boil with the following spices. Tie in a piece of muslin, 1 teaspoon juniper berries, 1 small piece nutmeg, 1 bay leaf, 1 teaspoon pepper corns, 4 cloves, 2 or 3 sprigs of thyme. Skim off any scum which comes to the top. Then boil five to ten minutes and leave to cool. Take the bag of spices out of the pan and put meat in (I use a small plastic dustbin for this purpose).

After three days the joint is ready to cook. I also use this brine when making a brawn or as we call it "Pork cheese", using $1/2$ a pig's head. Putting this in the above brine for three days. I then cook the pig's head in a large pan with the following ingredients:-

1 pig's trotter
1 medium sized onion
1 leek and 1 carrot
2 Bay leaves
2 sprigs of parsley
2 sprigs of thyme
6 peppercorns
2 tablespoons wine vinegar
Water to cover
(I also use $1/2$ a bottle of homemade Apple Wine and a little lemon juice)

Method

Boil altogether until the meat falls off the bones, but do not add lemon juice until the meat is cooked. The slower and steadier the meat cooks, the better. Keep tasting brawn before it sets, as food loses its flavour as it cools. After the liquid has been strained, keep back $1/2$ pint liquid with lemon juice. Cut up the meat into small pieces, boil another $1/2$ hour with liquid, lemon juice and Apple Wine. Pour into basins to set.

I often get asked for a recipe of the old-fashioned shortcakes. My mother used to make these most weeks to pack into my father's lunch box.

Old-fashioned Shortcakes

Ingredients
8 ozs self-raising flour
4 ozs lard and margarine (mixed)
3 ozs sugar

4 ozs currants or sultanas (sometimes, if mother had no dried fruit, she would cut dried prunes into small pieces and use these instead)
2 eggs

Method

Rub fat into flour, add sugar and fruit. Mix with eggs to a stiff dough (you may also need a little milk).

Roll out to $1/4$ inch thick and cut into oblong pieces. Mark with criss-crosses on top, paint with milk and sprinkle with sugar. Place on a flat baking tray and bake for 15-20 mins in oven at 325°F/170°C or Gas Mark 3.

Fleed Cakes

These cakes could be bought in the shops in the 1920s, sometimes spelt as Flead Cakes. It is the inside fat of a hog before it is melted into lard, and in those days pigs were widely bred in the country.

Ingredients

1lb S. R. flour
$1/2$ lb Fleed (Fleeds are flakes of pure lard)
$1/4$ lb butter
Pinch of salt

Method

Cut the fleeds into very small pieces. Mix flour and salt together. Rub in the fat and add the cut fleeds and mix well together. Add a little cold water to make a stiff dough. Flour the pastry board and roll out the dough, pressing hard on the rolling pin to press the fleeds well in. Flour the dough and cut into three strips, lay each of them on top of one another and roll up. Then roll flat again still using pressure on the roller. Repeat this three times, then roll out flat, about 1/4 inch thick, flour lightly and cut into squares, brush over with egg and milk and bake in a hot oven for 10-15 mins.

These cakes were cut in half and homemade jam spread on each half. Delicious they were, but I should imagine that they have far too many calories for eating them in these days.

HINTS FOR CHRISTMAS

1.   When holding a party put cling film over your best polished table to avoid water or wine marks from glasses.

2.   Cut down the smoke in the atmosphere from burning candles. Candles kept in the fridge for a few hours will burn more slowly.

3.   A cheap and non-alcoholic drink for drivers is soda water with a slice of lemon and a few drops of Angostura bitters.

4.   An inexpensive red wine, if left uncorked at room temperature for at least two hours will improve in taste.

5.   A teaspoon of glycerine added to royal icing stops it becoming too hard.

6.   Soak walnuts overnight in salty water, they will crack more easily without smashing the kernel inside the shell.

7.   Always store your nuts in a cold place as they become rancid extremely quickly if left in a warm atmosphere.

8.   Place Brazil nuts in a pan of cold water and bring to the boil ; after one minute plunge them back into cold water. You will find they shell more easily with their contents intact.

9.   If you have not made your Christmas pudding, mix it with cold tea instead of beer, as this gives a richer colour and stops it drying out.

10. If by chance the pudding turns out like a cannon-ball, slice it and fry it in butter and serve with sugar and cream.

11. The leftovers from the turkey seem to hang around for days. Try this old recipe, it's called **A Wet Devil.**

Take any pieces of cooked poultry, cover with mustard or any other pungent condiment and grill or heat in the oven. Make a sauce with the following ingredients:-

The juice of one lemon
A little red currant jelly
Cayenne pepper
1 dessertspoonful white sugar
$1/2$ teacup wine and
$1/2$ teacup ketchup or Worcestershire sauce
1 teacup gravy.

Method

Heat all together, then pour over the devilled poultry and serve very hot.

12. Cold turkey, ham or any other poultry can be put into a processor and mixed with a little salad cream or chutney, to be used as sandwich fillings.

13. Baked Potatoes. Place in hot oven for about one hour, cutting a cross on each with a sharp knife. Serve hot with strips of cold ham and turkey and a little chutney.

14. To give that boiling bacon extra flavour, add to the water, I teaspoon vinegar, 4 cloves and a little nutmeg.

15. Any spare almond paste left over from decorating the Christmas cake, can be used for stuffed dates. Just take the stones from the dates and fill in with almond paste.

16. Brandy butter can be served with mince pies or baked apples - it is surprising how long it will keep in an airtight jar.

17. Crystallised and glacé fruits - whole or broken pieces can be used for cake decoration or toppings for ice-cream. I also use stem ginger chopped and mixed in ice-cream and served with a chocolate sauce.

18. If you forgot to put charms in your Christmas pudding, wrap them in tin foil and put in the pudding whilst it is hot - the slits will soon close.

19. To prevent your Christmas candle dripping, put a little common salt around the top of the candle, before lighting - it should not drip at all.

SOME CHRISTMAS DRINKS

Punch is the perfect party drink and can be made in large amounts up to 2 hours beforehand. Mix all the ingredients and gently heat in a pan. One thing, never allow the punch to boil or you will lose some of the alcohol.

For a *Red Hot Punch* I use the following:- 1 bottle of any red wine (usually home-made); 3-4 tablespoons brandy; 3-4 tablespoons port; 1-litre lemonade; 1 lemon and 2 oranges, thinly sliced and a few cloves. Gently heat all the ingredients together and simmer for 15 minutes to infuse the flavour of the fruit. Serve hot, topped with fruit slices.

Cider Punch: 2 pints cider; 3 oranges, first stuck with cloves; 1 glass gin (size as liked). Put the oranges in the cider and gin and warm gently (not boiling). Serve hot.

Blackberry & Crab Apple Punch: 1 pint blackberry wine; 1 pint crab apples (or apple wine); 1 lemon and 1 orange, thinly sliced; 6 cloves; 1 teaspoon ground ginger; 1 teaspoon mixed spice; 1 teaspoon grated nutmeg; 12 ozs demerara sugar. Put all the ingredients into a large saucepan and almost bring to the boil, stirring all the while. Strain into a punch bowl and serve at once.

Christmas Cracker Punch: 2 pints red wine; I roasted lemon stuck with a dozen cloves; 8 ozs demerara sugar; 1 heaped teaspoon cinnamon; 2 oranges, thinly sliced. Roast the lemon stuck with cloves in a hot oven for about half an hour. Take from the oven and mix with the rest of the ingredients. Put into a large saucepan and bring almost to the boil. Strain, then float thinly sliced orange on top.

Colonel Negus: (Named after Colonel Negus of Queen Anne's day, who had a decided taste for sweet wine).

1 pint port; 4 ozs sugar; 1 lemon; pinch of nutmeg. Pour port into a bowl, add sugar, sliced lemon and nutmeg and let them float in the port. Pour in 2 pints of boiling water, mix well and serve hot.

If you want to make something for the children, try a Fruit Cup. Put fresh fruit, sliced, into a bowl, then pour in 1 pint lemonade and 1 pint orange juice. Mix and serve. You could always use blackcurrant and lemonade instead of orange juice and lemonade.

Liqueurs

Recipe 1

7 ozs whisky
12 ozs condensed milk
10 ozs single cream
3 teaspoons powdered coffee

Recipe 2

$1/2$ pint whisky
$1/2$ tin condensed milk
2 beaten eggs, size 3
$3/4$ carton single cream

1 tablespoonful chocolate powder or chocolate topping 1/2 tablespoon coffee powder

Method

Blend together. Leave for four days before drinking. Will keep for one month approximately in fridge. (If you are lucky!!). Shake before pouring.

Remember - homemade wines can be very high in alcohol, so have a taxi when going to a party. DON'T DRINK AND DRIVE.

Ginger Beer

Many cottages used to make their own beers. Ginger beer was a very popular drink. This is an old-fashioned recipe, which my mother used to make and as children we loved it - there were no cans of Coca-cola in my young days. Homemade lemonade was also very good. To make the ginger beer you need what countryfolk call a ginger beer plant.

To begin the plant you need $1^{1/2}$ cups of water, 2 teaspoons of ground ginger, 2 teaspoons of sugar. Place in a jar and feed with sugar and ginger. 2 teaspoons of ground ginger and 2 teaspoons of sugar every day for 7 days. If the water evaporates, add a little more. If this fails to produce little bubbles, then you will have to start again. On the seventh day the plant should be ready, so you can start to make ginger beer. Use 4 cups of sugar, dissolve with 10 cups of boiling water and 20 cups of cold water. Add well strained juice of 4 lemons. Now add the plant (which has been strained through a cloth until clean) to the above liquid. Mix and bottle. Let stand for 14 days when it is ready to drink. The plant is what is left in the straining cloth. Halve this and put it in a jar and start again with water and sugar and leave for 7 days. The other half can be thrown or given away, as only half the plant is needed.

Half a dozen puddings made from one recipe

I had this recipe given to me when I used to be on a weekly programme at Radio Orwell, called Peggy's Patch, and each week I used to give out a recipe. A listener to my programme rang in saying that she thought I might like to have this recipe, as it was such a useful one - and here it is :-

The foundation recipe is for a plain sponge pudding (you can always double up the ingredients if you want a larger pudding).

Ingredients and method

Rub $2^{1/2}$ ozs margarine into 6 ozs of self-raising flour, add a pinch of salt and 1 teaspoon of baking powder. Add 3 ozs of castor sugar. Add 1 beaten egg mixed with half a cupful of milk and stir it into the other ingredients. Pour into a well greased basin and steam for $1^{1/2}$ hours. Serve with jam or fruit purée sauce.

This admits of the following variations, when the sauce served would be custard or cream.

1.   After greasing the basin, put 3 tablespoons of raspberry jam in the base and pour the mixture over.

2. Line the basin with dates and pour the mixture over.

3. Mix a tablespoonful of cocoa with flour and two extra tablespoonfuls of milk.

4. Mix 2 ozs dessicated coconut with flour and other ingredients.

5. Flavour with strong black coffee or with coffee essence, and before putting the mixture into a basin, put in some halved, shelled walnuts.

6. Take some preserved ginger and cut up into pieces and add to the mixture.

❧

Years ago Sunday Tea was a special treat, when jellies and trifles were served. I don't think many people bother to make them these days, and they are regarded as a special treat. Children love jellies, and when we have a village function we always make sure there are plenty of jellies for them to eat, and they were a big hit when we had our VE Street Party.

But here is something different -

My Winter Trifle

Ingredients

12 ozs mixed dried fruit, apricots, apples etc.

2 *pints of water*
8 *Trifle sponge cakes*
Finely grated rind and juice of a lemon
3 *ozs sugar*
4 *tablespoons sweet sherry*
1 *pint of (made up) custard*
5 *ozs double cream*
A few flaked toasted almonds
3 *ozs preserved ginger (if liked)*

Method

Put fruit in a bowl, add 2 pints of water and leave to soak over night. Crumble the trifle sponges into the base of a 4 pint dish and put the soaked fruit into a pan with the liquid, lemon rind, juice and 3 ozs of sugar. Bring to the boil and simmer for 30 minutes or until tender. Remove from the heat, add sherry and chopped ginger. Allow to cool slightly, then spoon fruit and juice over sponge cakes. Meanwhile make up your pint of custard. Cool and pour over the fruit. Chill. Whip cream and spread over trifle. Sprinkle with almonds.

You will find this trifle a little different from the traditional one. By using dried fruit instead of tinned fruit you can use any dried fruit of your choice.

Another nice sweet to have at Christmas time, or the New Year, is Boozy Plums, and it is so simple to make.

Boozy Plums

Ingredients

1lb good quality dried prunes
2 tablespoons brown sugar
Cheap Ruby Wine or Port

Method

Place prunes in a jar with screw top, add sugar and fill the jar to the top with wine. Give it a stir each day for a fortnight. Serve fruit with ice-cream. You can also make another batch of prunes in the same juice, or you can drink the juice. I have also used homemade loganberry wine, as it's not so heavy.

As I write this cookbook, we have just had our VE Day Celebrations, and I was given a recipe for a 1942 Christmas Cake. With rations so short, these were all the ingredients we had to make the cake with:-

Wartime Christmas Cake

Ingredients

9 ozs plain flour
3 ozs finely chopped carrots
3 ozs fat

5-6 ozs dried fruit
2 ozs sugar
$1^{1}/_{2}$ level teaspoonfuls of ground cinnamon or mixed spice
1 level teaspoon of bicarbonate soda 1 tablespoon of Golden Syrup
1 small teaspoon of vinegar
Milk to moisten
(Note there are no eggs in this recipe)

Method

Prepare the fruit, using whatever may be available. Sift the flour into a mixing bowl with bicarbonate of soda and spice. Rub in the fat and stir in the prepared fruit and sugar and mix together. Make a well in the centre of the mixture and add the grated carrots. Warm the Golden Syrup slightly and stir in, adding sufficient milk to moisten and mix all together. Lastly, add the vinegar, stir it quickly into the mixture and pour into a greased cake tin. Bake at once in a very moderate oven for about $1^{1}/_{4}$ to $1^{1}/_{2}$ hours.

The next recipe is rather different, and what I call a boozy Christmas Cake not good for the figure!

Boozy Christmas Cake

Ingredients

$1^{1}/_{2}$lb currants
1lb sultanas
8 oz mixed chopped peel
4 oz ground almonds

¹/2 pint brandy or sherry
1lb 2 oz plain flour
1 teaspoon mixed spice
6 eggs
4 oz glacé cherries
1lb butter
1lb castor sugar
1 tablespoon treacle
A little milk if required

Method

Put the clean dried fruit into a large bowl and pour over the sherry. Allow to stand for at least 24 hours, stirring occasionally. Then put to one side and cover with a cloth. Sieve the flour and spice together and beat in the eggs. Cut the cherries into quarters, cream butter and sugar and add the treacle and beat all together thoroughly. Add a little flour and the eggs alternately and all the remaining ingredients in small amounts, folding in in between each addition. Mix to a dropping consistency, using a little milk if necessary. Turn into a greased lined 10 inch square cake tin and bake slowly for 5 to 6 hours at 140°C/275°F or Gas Mark 1. Cover with greaseproof paper if the surface starts to brown too much. Leave in the tin to cool. You can use half the ingredients to make a smaller cake, using a 7 inch square cake tin and baking for 4¹/2 hours.

I have been very lucky over the years and have met some wonderful people. I often wonder what my working class parents would have thought if they could have known that their daughter would mix and talk with Royals, Lords and Ladys! Lady Penn, whose late husband, Sir Eric, was an Equerry to the Queen, used to live at Stenfield House near Saxmundham. Lady Penn is a close friend of Princess Margaret and over the years she has been very kind to me. I last met Princess Margaret at the 1995 Suffolk Show. When she was asked if she remembered me, she walked over and chatted to me, just like she did the time she visited my garden in August 1983. She asked if I still opened my garden, and also asked how I was keeping. I wanted to say that I had met her sister, the Queen, a year ago, when I went to Buckingham Palace to receive my M.B.E., but I was so nervous and was at a loss for words. Lady Penn now lives in Scotland and has given me her Scottish Recipe for Butter Shortbread.

Lady Penn's Butter Shortbread

Makes 8 large pieces or 12 smaller, which I prefer.

Ingredients

6 oz plain flour
Pinch of salt
2 oz castor sugar
4 oz butter
Castor sugar to dredge

Method

Grease an oven baking tray and place a 7 inch greased flan ring on it. Sift together the flour and salt (I sieve the flour first to lighten it, and then mix the flour, caster sugar and salt quickly in the Magimix to blend them). I then cut the butter into small pieces and add it to the dry mixture in the bowl and run the machine for a short time, just long enough to form, a light dough. (This can be done by hand by kneading lightly). I then tip it into the flan ring, and press it down. Then I prick it with a fork all over. Bake in an oven set at 170°C (I use a fan oven at 150°C) for about 40 minutes until light golden brown.

Lift off the flan ring and sprinkle with caster sugar and mark while warm into 8 or 12 portions with a knife.

When slightly cooled cut into pieces and place on a wire rack. If you leave it to cool too much it will break when you cut it. When completely cold store in an airtight container.

I have an Aga, but this is better baked in an electric cooker.

A few years ago I met the Duchess of Devonshire at the Chelsea Flower Press Day. She is a charming lady and I felt very honoured when she gave me an interview for Radio Orwell and talked to me about her roses - one thing we had in common is a love of roses.

After all these years, the Duchess of Devonshire has again come into my life with a contribution for my book. Evelyn Curtis, my agent, secretary and general factotum found a most unusual chocolate cake recipe in Lady Maclean's Cook Book, which was given to Lady Maclean by the Duchess of Devonshire. Evelyn wrote to both these ladies and they kindly agreed to let me use this recipe in my book, and here it is.

Chocolate Cake

$1/2$lb butter beaten to a cream

7 egg yolks and whites beaten separately The whites stirred in last $1/2$lb bitter or vanilla chocolate scraped down and heated in the

oven, then beaten into the butter with 3 oz flour. $^{1/}2$lb sifted sugar 4 oz pounded almonds 1 teaspoon salvolatile.

This cake must be baked in a slow oven. It is better when eaten two days' old, and a thin icing of sugar keeps it moist. The teaspoon of salvolatile ingredient makes the cake unusual, and it is said by the Duchess of Devonshire, to complement the flavour of the chocolate, and having tried it out I believe it does!

Special Mince Pies

Prepare shortcrust pastry, adding grated rind of 1 orange to 8 oz of flour and mixing it with the juice of an orange instead of water.

Roll out the pastry and cut into pie cases, line pastry tins and put one teaspoonful of mincemeat into each little pie. Top with a mixture of 4 oz cream cheese and 1 oz caster sugar. Mix together, using one small teaspoonful on top of the mincemeat. Then cover with pastry lid in the usual way.

There is an old saying - "first mince pie, one should have a wish", so here's wishing you all success with my recipes and my thanks to all my friends who have given me their favourite ones.

Index

Angelica stalks, crystallised,	34	Damson & Walnut Jam,	113
Apple Ale,	85	Damson,	112
Apple Charlotte,	52-53	Danish Apple Pudding,	85-86
Apricot & Almond Pie,	81	Dumplings (hard and soft),	17-18
Banana & Walnut Cake,	51-52	Eggs, coloured, decorating of,	36
Banana Chartreuse,	102-103	Elder Rob,	88
Banana Slice,	41-42	Elderflower Champagne,	53-54
Bay,	60	Elderflower Cordial,	54
Bean & Cabbage Salad,	45	Fish & Apple Bake,	74
Beer Pickle,	132-133	Fish Pie,	37-38
Bible Cake,	121-123	Fleed Cakes,	135-136
Black Cherry Wine,	75	Flowers, edible,	62-63
Blackberry & Apple Jam,	109		
Blackcurrant Vinegar,	88	Ginger,	119-120
Boozy Christmas Cake,	147-148	Gingered Pears,	73
Boozy Plums,	146	Gooseberry & Mint Jelly,	59
Bread & Butter Pickle,	126-127	Gooseberry Wine,	77-78
Cauliflower Cheese,	37	Half A Dozen Puddings from	
Cauliflower Soufflé,	36-37	One Recipe,	143-144
Cheese Cakes,	65	Hazelnut Meringue,	111
Cheese Scotch Eggs,	64	Hazelnut Pie with Vegetables,	112
Cherry Brandy,	76	Hazelnuts,	110-111
Chestnut Soup,	14	Herb and Vegetable Remedies,	56-57
Chocolate Cake,	150-151	Herbal Vinegars,	88-89
Christmas, drinks for,	140	Herbs, oils and vinegars,	61
Christmas, hints for,	137-139	Herbs, preserving and freezing,	62
Cobblestone Cake,	47	Horseradish,	120-121
Coffee Pudding with Chocolate			
Hazelnut Sauce,	39-40	Jill's Chocolate Roulade,	101-102
Country Flan,	44	Joan's Scalloped Potato Dish,	43
Country hints,	94-95		
Courgette Omelette,	118-119	Lady Penn's Butter Shortbread,	149-150
Crab Apple Jelly,	106-108		
Cream, use of,	91-92	Leeky Stew with Nacker Jack,	18-19
		Loganberry Wine,	76-77

Index

Marmalade,	22-23
Meat & Potato Pie,	98-99
Medlar Jam,	131
Medlars,	130-131
Merryweather,	112
Mincemeat Cake,	104
Mint remedies,	58
Mixed Fruit Chutney,	130
Mixed Nut Pudding,	43
Mushroom Ketchup,	90
Old Fashioned Shortcakes,	134-135
Parsley, growing of,	33-34
Parsnip Chips,	19 -20
Parsnip Fritter,	20
Pavlova,	70
Pea Soup,	14
Pear Chutney,	129
Peggy's Chocolate Soufflé,	99-100
Pickled Mushrooms,	109-110
Pigeon Casserole,	48-49
Pigeon Pudding	49
Pineapple Carrot Cake,	49-51
Plum & Marshmallow Pie,	71-72
Poor man's asparagus,	131
Poor Man's Brandy,	24
Potato Cakes,	20 -21
Preserved Ginger,	119-120
Preserves and jams, country,	106-109
Puff ball,	110
Pumpkin & Cream Cheese Pâté	115
Pumpkin Bread,	117-118
Pumpkin Cheesecake,	116
Pumpkin Pickle,	115-116

Punch,	
Blackberry & Crab Apple,	140
Christmas Cracker,	140
Cider,	140
Colonel Negus,	140-141
Red Hot,	140
Quick brine,	133-134
Quince Jelly,	114
Quince,	113-114
Raspberry Vinegar,	87-88
Rhubarb, pie and turnover,	26
Rice Wine,	23-24
Rich Potato bake,	123-125
Rose Vinegar,	78
Rosemary,	60
Rosewater,	78
Sage,	61
Samfer,	131
Samphire,	131
Simnel Cake,	32-33
Singing Johnny (liqueur),	105
Sloe & Apple Jelly,	108-109
Soft fruit,	69
Special Mince Pies,	151
Spicy Malt Loaf Cake,	6,9
Spicy Tea Cake,	28
Spinach Salad,	46
Stilton Dip,	63-64
Strawberry Cheesecake,	72
Strawberry Tart,	79-80
Stuffed Onions,	16-17

Index

Suffolk Rusks, 66
Suffolk Sausage, 96-97
Swede, 125
Swedes with Bacon, 125-126
"Sweet Treat" Scottish Tablet, 104

Three Fruit Chutney, 116
Toffee Apples, 86-87
Tomato & Red Pepper Chutney, 128
Tomato, 128

Vegetables, 56

Walnut Tray Bake, 27
Walnuts, pickled, 83-84
Wartime Christmas Cake, 147-148
Watercress Spread, 35
Wet Devil, 138
Winter Trifle, 144-145